I Never Loved a Man the Way I Love You

I Never Loved a Man the Way I Love You

Aretha Franklin, Respect, and the Making of a Soul Music Masterpiece

MATT DOBKIN

ST. MARTIN'S PRESS ✻ NEW YORK

www.stmartins.com

Copyright permissions appear on page 245.

Book design by Jonathan Bennett

Library of Congress Cataloging-in-Publication Data

Dobkin, Matt.
    I never loved a man the way I love you: Aretha Franklin, respect, and the making of a soul music masterpiece/Matt Dobkin.
        p. cm.
    Includes discography (p. 227) and index (p. 247).
    ISBN 0-312-31828-6
    EAN 978-0-312-31828-4
    1. Franklin, Aretha. 2. Soul musicians—United States—Biography. I. Title.

ML420.F778D63 2004
782.421644'092—dc22
[B]   2004051139

First Edition: November 2004

10   9   8   7   6   5   4   3   2   1

For Charles Runnette and for Allyson Pimentel

contents

Foreword

A Song for Me

by Nikki Giovanni

This is what I remember: Aretha Franklin was booked to perform at the Cincinnati Cotton Club for one whole week. I didn't have the money to go, nor was it likely my parents would let me if I could earn the ticket price, but it was nonetheless exciting. She cancelled the day after she arrived. They said she was sick. We learned later she was pregnant, which is not a sickness. I am just about a year younger than Lady Soul. I thought they simply should have said: Aretha Franklin is expecting and is going home to be with her family. But those were the days—the early 1960s—when things like that took on other meanings. Aretha had written, "What is romance without the one you love?" I was sixteen. I just wanted to know what is romance.

It must have been the blues that made Aretha mean so

much to everybody. Maybe she caught a cold when she was an infant and her mother or grandmother rubbed her chest with oil of cloves. Something like that must have given her voice that smoldering quality. Maybe it was the jowl bacon in the pinto beans with a side of cold water corn bread, or maybe fried fish with hush puppies. There had to be okra 'cause she lived with Mahalia Jackson, so there must have been stewed okra with tomatoes or just good old collard greens with a splash of hot vinegar. Fried chicken. I couldn't have forgotten the fried chicken. Try Matty's, she said. And we all did.

Ellis Haizlip, the producer of *Soul!*, the first variety Black television show on PBS, invited me to go see Aretha at the Apollo Theatre in Harlem. Honi Coles was the official greeter then. I recognized him immediately but was surprised that he greeted me by name. Aretha brought the house down! After the show Ellis asked if I'd like to meet her. He knew I had written a poem and asked, "Did you bring a copy for her?" "Absolutely not!" was my response. What if she didn't like it? What if she thought it was an intrusion? What if—too many things that would make me very nervous. I have, I must admit, only limited social skills anyway. What would I say to her? And she to me? I have never written poetry about people I know because I never have wanted anyone to think I would take advantage of access. Only three people that I have written about have

I actually met. But I couldn't not go backstage. I would rather have died to have her think I was there and so disrespectful. So I met Aretha.

When she played Lincoln Center a few years later I decided to give myself an early birthday present. I purchased a block of tickets: three in the front, three in the middle, and three in the back, like a Rubik's Cube. As the day of the show came I started to feel guilty. I had started out not wanting anyone to sit next to me, but then it dawned on me that Aretha would look out—these were orchestra seats in the Philharmonic—and see empty seats and might think people either hadn't bought the tickets or didn't bother to come. I gave the three back seats to my students but kept the rest. I just couldn't resist it. She came out cooking! Then you know how after that second number or so she took a breath. She walked to the edge of the stage and said, "Hi, Nikki." Then went on with the show. I was so totally thrilled! I'm still all smiles about it.

Aretha's youngest boy and my only son both attended Emerson when she lived on the Upper East Side. We were West Siders at Ninety-second and Columbus. The bus went through the park at Ninety-third or Ninety-fourth, coming out almost exactly at Emerson. Thomas wasn't really old enough to ride the bus by himself, but some days I would allow him to ride by himself by calling the school and asking them to look out for him. Most days either

Debbie, his baby-sitter, or I would take him. One day, when I was with him, the headmistress asked if she could get some advice from me. She wanted to do a fund-raiser and wondered if Aretha would be a part of it. My advice: Ask her. I didn't know Aretha, I had only met her, but her commitments were pretty clear. She had offered to pay Angela Davis's bail. She had been a steady foot soldier for Dr. King. She is one superstar who has, it seems to me, always stayed on the case. Sometimes in front, sometimes behind the scene, but always there.

Then one evening my phone rang. "Nikki, this is Aretha. Are you busy?" First of all, there are two female voices that are totally distinct: Aretha's and Lena Horne's. They can't disguise their voices even if they want to. I grabbed a cup of coffee to chat. She was back at the Apollo and I had, as always, seen and loved the show. Why didn't you come backstage? I didn't want to be in your way. Did I play the piano too much? Should I keep it in the act? You could play the piano all night. I wish you'd make an album of only piano playing. (I still would love that.) For a brief time, tied together by what Carolyn Rodgers calls the "witch cord," we were two career women trying to make sense of it all. I talked with her only once after that. A magazine editor and I were at her home to interview her. Her people were there being very protective, and I sort of laughed to myself because I'm very protective of Aretha's gentle and fragile spirit, too. She showed us her home and we settled in the kitchen to talk. But there was some sort of fog, some sort of heavy blanket that wouldn't let the words come through. Writers are not to be trusted. We can sometimes turn words around, tie meanings to events that are not accurate. I didn't want to see Aretha not able to re-lax so we soon left, writing the article more from press re-leases than from what she had said.

I was in Detroit recently and saw Aretha's cousin Brenda and remembered, with her, the evening we were onstage after the show was over and the audience had gone home. Aretha sat down at the piano and began singing. Brenda offered background vocals. I was just there listening: to a song for me.

"I don't know *anybody* that can sing a song like Aretha Franklin. Nobody. Period."

—RAY CHARLES, 1968

one

"The Voice of Black America"

*L*ast fall I went to an Aretha Franklin concert at Radio City Music Hall in New York City, not without some trepidation. As a lifelong Aretha fan in possession of thirty-eight of her albums, I knew to be wary: Although her almost otherworldly vocal prowess was inarguable, her shows, over the years, had become maddeningly hit-or-miss. The singer was notorious for showing up with a corps of luridly attired dancers, Aretha herself in some sort of impossibly unflattering get-up, looking more like a Las Vegas nightclub chanteuse as *MAD TV* might conceive one than like the universally revered Queen of Soul. Her song selection could be dubious and might rear its head at any moment, consigning her audience to an evening of treacle like "People" and "The Greatest Love of All," rather than soul stalwarts like "Do Right Woman" and "Chain of Fools." Other times, Aretha would show up at the theater just flat-out not in the mood, her desire to get offstage palpable, her devotion to the crowd not the equal of theirs to her.

But this time, Aretha was *present*. And when Aretha is there—committed, impassioned, emotionally involved in her songs—there's nothing else like it in all of music. Her sublime vocalism, almost preternaturally full of feeling and operatic in size, is supported by a kind of immaculate musicality and innate sense of improvisational rightness. As her longtime producer Jerry Wexler puts it, "There are three qualities that make a great singer—head, heart, and throat. The head is intelligence, the phrasing. The heart is the emotionality that feeds the flames. The throat is the chops, the voice. Ray Charles certainly has the first two. Aretha, though, like Sam Cooke, has all three qualities. Her gift seems to have sprung, like Minerva, full-fledged from Jupiter's head."

The gift—forceful, emotional, unpredictable—was certainly in evidence that night at Radio City, as was a kind of comprehensive curatorial care with regards to the set list. Aretha, sixty-one at the time, was clad in a glimmering white gown encrusted with rhinestones, a white organza shawl draped over her shoulders. A long, straight (and synthetic) ponytail cascaded from the very top of her head almost to her waist. She opened the show singing "Won't Be Long," a song she recorded for her first album for Columbia Records when she was eighteen years old. She paid further tribute to her oft-maligned (to a large degree, unfairly so) tenure at Columbia with a poignant "If Ever I Would Leave You" and an ethereal "Skylark," a longstanding Johnny Mercer/Hoagy Carmichael favorite of Aretha's that she has recorded several times over her career. The musical highpoint of the show was a deep, bluesy "Dr. Feelgood," with Franklin seated at the piano—where she belongs—pounding out the gospel-inflected chords of her composition and giving them the kind of resonant bottom than can't be matched on a recording.

It was during this song that Aretha seemed most herself, most palpably the "natural woman" she came to embody, in the eyes of both black and white America, in the late 1960s. As she eased her way into "Dr. Feelgood," banging out an extended piano introduction, she suddenly paused and announced, "I feel like letting it all hang out tonight." With that she tore off the temporary ponytail dramatically and tossed it onto the piano with a flourish, leaving a short, sad little stump of real hair in its place. The move would become a Franklin signature this particular season (she would reprise it in a televised BET tribute honoring her career), but it nevertheless had an impact, and the crowd roared. Shedding this part of her costume, reminding us that she was both superstar and ordinary woman with a weave, was the perfect symbol of Aretha's combination of awesome talent and down-to-earth "realness," an attribute Franklin prizes almost above all others. Aretha loves her designer gowns and isn't above throwing in a piece of campy razzle-dazzle to lend her act a touch of showmanship—but always while grounded in her own sense of authenticity. Her shows can be either over-the-top or underwhelming, but they are fundamentally rooted in Aretha's own, very personal notion of what her singing is about: "me, with my hand outstretched, hoping someone will take it."

The concert wound down, and as Aretha dispensed with the obligatory thank-yous to her band and backup singers, a personal slide show commenced on an enormous screen overhead. Here was Aretha with Mary J. Blige; Aretha in miles of mink at Bill Clinton's inauguration; super-thin Aretha after one of her successful diets in the 1970s. Most of the shots were in color and relatively recent. The audience collectively craned their necks to observe but seemed relatively unmoved.

Until, that is, one particular, striking image was projected, almost shockingly, above our heads. Dating from February 1968, the photo was taken at Detroit's official "Aretha Franklin Day" and captured, in evocative black-and-white, the singer in a shapeless dress, with a band of feathers up around the chin and another around the hips, constructed out of what looked to be a rather hot, uncomfortable fabric. Her hair was in the de rigueur bouffant style of the era, the eye makeup Egyptian, and she clutched a plaque commemorating the occasion. Beside her, grinning happily, seemingly thrilled to be present at what was essentially a publicity op for a beleaguered Midwestern city and its favorite daughter, was Martin Luther King, Jr. The reverend was in his customary dark suit, white shirt, and dark tie; what was unusual was the sense of casual joy projected by the man so often portrayed in photos and film clips as solemn, burdened by the weight of his work. The image had the patina of history about it: Aretha and Martin instantly and palpably evoked an iconic sixties, a moment in time that indeed seems to exist in black-and-white in the collective memory. A moment when the country, uncharacteristically, seemed to be heeding the advice of one of the last tracks Aretha had recorded for Columbia Records a year or so earlier, "Take a Look," which exhorted: "Take a look in the mirror/Look at yourself/But don't you look too close . . . Lord, what's happening to this human race? I can't even see one friendly face. . . ." Perhaps only a shot of Martin with Kennedy or Martin with Muhammad Ali could have summoned that decade more swiftly or completely.

The event was held in Detroit's Cobo Hall exactly a year after "Respect" had hit the airwaves. Aretha was receiving awards from both *Cash Box* magazine, for a year's worth of pop-chart ubiquity, and from King's Southern Christian Leadership Conference, honoring the work the singer had done for the civil rights movement for much of the previous decade. In addition to King, Aretha's sisters were present, as was her father, the Reverend C. L. Franklin, a well-known preacher who had introduced Martin to Detroit for that city's 1963 civil rights march, which would serve as a template for King's famous march on Washington later that year. For those of us who followed Aretha's career closely, the picture was familiar, but the moment it appeared, the Radio City audience erupted in cheers and whoops. Several people started to cry. *This* was who her fans believed Aretha to be. Aretha, in black-and-white, standing with the man who was similarly emblematic of an era and an ideal—*this* was the real Aretha: a woman who in the space of a year had captured the public imagination and become the queen of the pop charts at the same time as she came to be viewed as what the poet Nikki Giovanni calls "the voice of the civil rights movement, the voice of black America." This was the Aretha who was born not out of Jupiter's skull but from the offices of Atlantic Records with the 1967 release of her breakthrough album *I Never Loved a Man the Way I Love You*. Mere months later, Aretha would sing at a King memorial service. But at this moment in February 1968, she was civil rights activist, icon of black womanhood, the most respected popular singer in the world. It is this freeze-frame Aretha that I've tried to capture.

The "masterpiece" referred to in the title of this book is not "Respect," although that song certainly had something to do with it. Otis Redding's classic, as reimagined, rere-corded, and, most importantly, re-*sung* by Aretha Franklin, is an anthem (a "battle cry," Aretha calls it), a call-to-arms for women, civil rights activists, and, of course, the lovelorn. "I once called 'Respect' a combination of a global sororal call to fraternity—or sorority—combined with personal lubricity," Jerry Wexler told me. For other listeners who felt the racial implications of the song more forcefully than its feminist-sexual undercurrents, "Respect" was the sound of revolution.

But "Respect" is just one part of a larger work of art of even greater breadth and influence. The album that gar-nered the singer her first major hits, *I Never Loved a Man* was a pop- and soul-music milestone for Aretha, but apart from its status as a hit record, Aretha's Atlantic debut also secured a wider cultural import beyond the scope of the *Billboard* charts almost immediately upon its release. The Civil Rights Movement had long been in full swing; now it had its theme song. Five years before Gloria Steinem launched *Ms.* magazine, feminists had their song too.

I Never Loved a Man the Way I Love You, acknowledged

1

by virtually every major music survey as among the best albums of the rock era (the *New York Times* said it "sounds like freedom"), won Aretha the first of her seventeen Grammys (one of which was for Lifetime Achievement; the most recent of which she was awarded in February 2004). In 1994 she received a Kennedy Center Honor; in 1987 she had already become the first woman to be inducted into the Rock and Roll Hall of Fame. Lady Soul has received no shortage of accolades. Yet her monumental contribution to popular music, today, is not taken seriously by a large sector of the public. Dubious taste in clothes and material, a limited performance schedule (thanks to a crippling fear of flying), and a certain divalike imperiousness (the product more of a natural shyness than of arrogance) have conspired to make Franklin come across more as a soul-sista caricature than as the genre-crossing, unclassifiable genius that she is. What's more, the extent of her vocal gift is often taken for granted; the fact that she's a great singer is almost a cliché, something people reflexively know without stopping to ponder why or how. Women singers, no matter how gifted, habitually get short shrift with regard to other elements of their musicality. Aretha is a great singer not just because of her instantly recognizable tone but because of her vocal flexibility, her interpretive intelligence, her skillful piano-playing, her ear, her experience.

I Never Loved a Man the Way I Love You is the title for this book not just because it's the title of the album in question but because it nicely raises the question of the exact identity of "you." Who is Aretha singing to, on this album and indeed in all of her music? The potential answers to this question summon various key themes in the singer's life. When she sings the words "I never loved a man the way I love you," is Aretha speaking to a man at all, or to God? The influence of Aretha's gospel training on her subsequent art cannot be overstated. Her formative years were spent learning her art in the church—for much of her life, consequently, music *was* the praising of the Lord. Along with Ray Charles, Aretha is largely responsible for bringing to the pop charts the kind of fervent, transcendent singing that had previously only existed in black churches. The gospel undertones of all her recorded output suggest that, when performing some particularly inspired vocal feat, Aretha could potentially be addressing either a lover or the Lord, a sex/religion paradox she picked up from Ray Charles and passed on to artists like Al Green and Marvin Gaye.

The lyric might also refer to Aretha's preacher father, to whom Aretha's devotion was without limits; there was nothing she wouldn't do for the famous and charismatic C. L. Franklin, a celebrity in his own right in the black church, an influential preacher whose musical delivery was widely imitated, and by most accounts a loving yet strict, demanding, and authoritative parent. Is Aretha swearing fealty to Daddy when she sings "I never loved a man the way I love you"? Certainly, lovers came in and out of the singer's life; her love for her father, however, was constant.

That said, the words of this song could of course refer to any number of the men in Aretha's life. At fourteen, she gave birth to her first child; she was no stranger to the coarser sex when she recorded this album at age twenty-four. Aretha herself has said, "If I can't feel it, I can't sing it," so we can confidently assume that some element of her personal life was being limned in her performance of the album's title cut (and indeed in all of her songs). Is "you" then-husband Ted White with whom Aretha had an undeniably stormy marriage? Could "you" be the still-unnamed father of Aretha's first child, or some other early lover of the singer? ("I think you have to bring it down to something carnal," Nikki Giovanni told me.)

When Aretha sings, "I never loved a man the way I loved you" (or, for that matter, when she sings, "you make me feel like a natural woman" or, "you better think about what you're trying to do to me" or, "ain't no way for me to love you, if you won't let me"), I for one feel as if she's singing directly to me. And this is the facet of Aretha's talent that I've tried to uncover. Whatever she sings, Aretha is nothing if not defiantly direct, open, real. At the height of her powers, Aretha's voice was fundamental, essential, honest, her presence complete, convincing, inarguable. As Robert Christgau, longtime music critic of the *Village Voice,* has written of Aretha's singing, "Its power is so ineffable that no one has ever satisfactorily described it in words. One reason the sentimental myths that identify her solely with soul grit and gospel exaltation hold such sway is that they at least make surface sense." But what's below the surface? How to describe the voice's melding of sweetness, sass, sex, pain, and strength, plus a metaphysical element, something unknowable? The challenge in writing about Aretha is to describe the essence of her voice, to go beyond the surface analysis described by Christgau, which so far has had to suffice when examining her art.

Aretha Franklin is *not* a diva. Although endless television specials, magazine tributes, critical commentary, homages from colleagues and other forms of contemporary mythmaking have conspired to persuade us in recent years that a diva is a "strong woman" of talent and Aretha is their queen, the truth is that Aretha, like her uncategorizable vocal gift, cannot be shoehorned into a shorthand designation co-opted from the world of opera for marketing purposes. If she comes across as imperious, it's in large part because she's shy; if she seems competitive with younger singers toward whom it would be more becoming

11

to act as a mentor, it's because Aretha has bouts of insecurity. Her voice may be larger than life, but Aretha herself is not. "Natural woman" gets to the heart of the matter, but "ordinary woman" may even be more like it. To understand Aretha's universal appeal, it's essential to consider not just The Voice, but the woman behind it.

Conventional wisdom holds that Aretha's unprecedented international success with her first few Atlantic albums was the direct result of having been brought "back to church" by Jerry Wexler, being allowed to apply her gospel vocals and gospel pianism to material aimed at a mainstream pop audience. This is certainly true, but it's only part of the story. Aretha's very first, John Hammond–produced (and hitless) Columbia album contains several numbers of a decidedly gospel cast. "Are You Sure?" for example, is explicit in its Lord-praising message, as Aretha encourages her listeners to try prayer as a means of coping with daily travails and getting closer to the Lord. And even pop standards like "Over the Rainbow" were given the gospel treatment, with Aretha's impassioned wails lending "The Shoop Shoop Song," "You Made Me Love You," "Ac-cent-tchu-ate the Positive" and other such middle-of-the-road fare an emotionality and ferocity that had never been heard before, certainly not from the female pop vocalists who traditionally essayed such material.

No, the novelty of Aretha's first Atlantic releases, the element that pushed her into the popular-music stratosphere was not gospel fervor (though that certainly helped). It was sex. Even on a childhood gospel album, recorded when she was fourteen years old, Aretha sings with an uncanny world-weariness, but her early Columbia recordings were decidedly girlish, almost coy. When at Columbia she sang of searching for "a meadow in the mist, where someone's waiting to be kissed," there was longing in her voice, but it was a kind of inchoate yearning not necessarily identifiable as wholly sexual. From "Do Right Woman" to "Dr. Feelgood" to "Respect" to the title track, on the other hand, *I Never Loved a Man the Way I Love You* is an album largely about female sexual desire, a subject previously owned by the blues women of the early part of the century. It wasn't just reclaiming a style with which she'd previously praised the Lord that made Aretha essential; it was using that style and marrying it to the blues in order to portray her needs as a real woman that positioned her as inheritor to the mantle of Bessie Smith and Billie Holiday and turned her into a superstar. Diana Ross and the Supremes had been churning out hits on the pop charts for several years. But no female singer had yet emerged as a bona fide recording artist, directing the action in the studio, producing cohesive album-length works, until Aretha showed the world that forty-one minutes (eleven tracks) of church-influenced soul music could be considered a thematically consistent and lasting work of passion and craftsmanship. Even figures like Holiday and Ella Fitzgerald, though rightly revered for their musicianship, were largely viewed as "chick singers." Not so Aretha, circa 1967. But getting that passion—that soul—on wax didn't happen without a few hitches along the way.

two

Three White Men

1966

Jerry Wexler wanted to sell the company. The forty-nine-year-old producer had been with Atlantic Records for thirteen years, ever since the label founder, the youngish Turk Ahmet Ertegun, had poached him from a job hawking second-rate tunes for a music publisher, capitulating to the industry neophyte's brash demand for a partnership stake in the company. For more than a dozen years Wex had worked obsessively, demandingly, some might say pugnaciously, as record exec, A&R man and producer, enjoying to the fullest a job that indulged his longstanding passion for black music. It also had provided him with enough show-business anecdotes (a priceless perk for the incorrigible raconteur) to last a lifetime: being forced to stack desks in Atlantic's first, tiny office in order to clear space for a makeshift "studio"; making pilgrimages to black sections of sharply segregated New Orleans where white faces were seldom glimpsed (and almost never fondly) to track down a singer he and Ertegun had caught wind of; sweating in his suit as a district attorney questioned him in connection with the payola scandal that rocked the record industry in the early sixties; plying a little-known Wilson Pickett with Jack Daniels in an effort to get him to write some original songs—and getting "In the Midnight Hour" for his trouble.

But by 1966, Wexler was convinced that Atlantic had reached an impasse. It was a company known first and foremost for its rhythm-and-blues artists, and Wex suspected that soul music was headed for an inevitable decline. Ahmet Ertegun himself was cultivating an interest in white British rock music, and his brother, Nesuhi, also a majority holder in the company, was primarily a jazz fanatic; were these genres in which Atlantic could dependably be counted on to excel? Tastes, both inside and outside the company, were shifting away from Wexler's bread and butter. The time to get out was now.

In many ways it made sense that Wexler was eager to cash in. Jerry had grown up in Washington Heights a tough Jewish kid of the Tin Pan Alley–loving, stickball-playing variety. To say that Jerry—the son of an immigrant window-washer and a housewife—had no firsthand knowledge of wealth is an understatement. The closest he had gotten to the high life was when he helped his father on his window-washing route and found himself staring through the glass into opulent apartments from a scaffold on the outside of the building. Despite the support and attentions of a devoted mother with an unshakable faith in her son's future greatness, Wexler's prospects had always looked dim. "I was a cosmic fuck-up," the man recalls of his early days, in a characteristically blunt yet metaphysical turn of phrase. As a teenager and into his twenties, he took on a variety of odd jobs (liquor store clerk, Catskills waiter) and even tried his hand at writing (at mother Elsa's prompting). But, he says, "The truth is I wasn't much of a worker or much of a writer."

That all changed when Jerry's professional life began to follow his personal passion: jazz. Wex's indoctrination into the world of jazz dates back to his childhood and teen years, a large swath of which was spent in a Washington Heights pool hall with a radio perpetually tuned to the latest swing hits. Was there a single male hipster in 1930s New York City who *wasn't* addicted to the riotous appearances around town of Fletcher Henderson, whose shows invariably afforded the opportunity to dance to the hottest new numbers and flirt with the cutest girls? When there was no gig to attend, Jerry and his buddies were ensconced at the Commodore Music Shop, owned by legendary record salesman and label owner Milt Gabler, where Wex radiated in the glow cast by another store regular, Columbia Records producer John Hammond ("I wouldn't dare approach him. It was like approaching Muhammad Ali."), and where he first conceived the farfetched notion that making jazz records might be something he, too, could do. "We were all fans of antiquarian jazz—Louis Armstrong, Jelly Roll Morton, Bessie Smith," Wexler remembers. "And we banded together and did something nobody does anymore: we sat around and listened to records—communally." The other thing they did communally was develop a fondness for that inevitable jazz-world accoutrement: "grass."

When Jerry wasn't toking up and listening to records, he was avidly devouring literature, a habit that, along with his mother's conviction that he was destined to produce the Great American Novel, crystallized a desire to write. After a stint in the army, Jerry urgently needed a steady-paying gig, and he set about turning his authorial fantasies into a practicable vocation. Before long, a friend got him a freelance gig writing promotional copy for BMI, AS-CAP's main rival in the music-publishing business. This led to a fulltime job at *Billboard*, then, as now, the industry bible, and it was there that Wexler made what's still his most noteworthy contribution to musical letters, the coining of the term "rhythm and blues," which he devised as an alternative to "race" records, a designation that even in the forties had unsavory social implications.

Wexler quickly took to churning out, on tight dead-
lines, vivid prose that benefited from his flair for colorful
characterization and that reflected his infatuation with
both high culture (he read Balzac, Turgenev, and Plato
contentedly and eventually built a significant collection of
surrealist paintings) and low (surrealism was even more
surreal if you were a prodigious pot-smoker). In his writing, he might use the word "Jew-boy" in one sentence and
"exiguous" in the next. Jerry is now eighty-seven, but his
verbal panache remains intact: When I visited him at his
home on Long Island to discuss *I Never Loved a Man*, he
apologized for being a bit tired, but the day before he had
endured a painful visit to the dentist: "Dental surgery is a
real motherfucker." I requested a follow-up interview the
next day, and he said, fancily, that it wouldn't be a problem: "You impinge on me most pleasantly."

When we met, Jerry and his wife, the author Jean
Arnold, were in the midst of selling their East Hampton
home, which they customarily used during the summer
months. They avoid the cold northeast winters at a lake-
side house in Sarasota, Florida. The house was airy and
comfortable with an attractive swimming pool out back,
which was being used by Jerry's daughter Lisa and a friend
while we talked. Jerry had decided, however, to move
down to Florida permanently; the back-and-forth was
getting to be too much. Spending just a little bit of time

with Jerry, it was easy to fathom that the effort required to maintain two homes more than a thousand miles apart was beyond his capabilities. Wex enjoys his reputation among music-business people as a tough SOB from the Bronx: In his heyday, he was a hulking, tall, physically imposing presence, with the kind of pronounced New York accent that's hard to believe still exists in the third millennium. The voice and the street savvy are still there, but, like most men approaching ninety, Jerry, though active, is frail. It took him some time to rip the cellophane off a blank VHS cassette so that he could tape the Yankees game while we had our interview. (An ardent sports fan, he wore a Yankees T-shirt both days I came to see him.) When we talked about some of his favorite artists who'd passed away, he faltered and asked that I turn off my tape recorder— particularly when we spoke about the supremely talented singer-pianist-composer Donny Hathaway, who committed suicide at age thirty-three, many believe because he was tormented by unresolved issues of sexuality. Brash, hardscrabble Jerry Wexler today is emotional in a way that's almost heartbreakingly poignant in old men. Yet, he's lost none of his acuity, and as we listened to the first album he made with Aretha Franklin, thirty-six years after it was recorded, his memory was remarkable, and his commentary illustrated the exceptional musical taste that made Wex one of the twentieth century's most respected producers, despite the fact that he never learned to play an instrument.

Throughout the sixties, Atlantic Records was regarded as the last word in rhythm and blues, but when Wexler arrived at the company in the early 1950s, the catalogue was surprisingly jazz-heavy, thanks in large part to the high-brow tastes of Nesuhi Ertegun. Dizzy Gillespie, Sarah Vaughan, Erroll Garner, Mary Lou Williams, Bobby Short (Bobby Short!)—all were, unbelievably, artists on the label that would eventually become home to Led Zeppelin. The real unit-mover, however, was Ruth Brown, whose hits "5-10-15 Hours" and "Mama, He Treats Your Daughter Mean" made the company look like a good fit for Jerry as he made the transition from reporting on records to making them. The down-home sass of a Ruth Brown—*this* was the direction Atlantic needed to go if it wanted to sell product, and both Wexler and Ahmet Ertegun were unabashed in their almost greedy desire to have hits, setting about the task with a conscious aim to make records that an audience of black adults would *need* to possess. It's hard to fathom in today's world, when pop music's target audience is comprised chiefly of twelve-year-old girls, that making music for economically disenfranchised rural blacks with families to feed was a shrewd business move. However, the appeal of Ruth Brown and, under Wexler's stewardship, LaVern Baker, Clyde McPhatter and Ray Charles, proved irresistible to the kind of consumer who thoroughly *depended* on soulful and diverting new music to get through the day. Indeed, at the height of the still-burgeoning soul movement, the songs on the R&B charts did much more than provide mere entertainment. In the midst of the tremendous social pressures of the sixties, many black Americans, both urban and in the country, needed powerful, gospel-trained voices to remind them that they had a place in the world. Referring to the music of Bobby "Blue" Bland and of Aretha Franklin, writer Mark Anthony Neal, in *What the Music Said: Black Popular Music and Black Public Culture,* asserts, "I didn't quite understand the hold that these sounds had on my father, as he sat entranced at the kitchen table, patting his feet, or how important this music was to his survival."

Wexler and Ertegun, if they didn't exactly understand this need, nevertheless welcomed such public reliance on soul-music heroes. "Our aim in 1966 was the same as it was in 1956 and 1976: to sell phonograph records in large quantities," Wexler says. "We were never a company with a long-term plan," Ertegun concurs. "We went from day to day. But we were aware of trends. We were in some turmoil because both Jerry and my brother wanted to sell the company. They were a bit older than I was and thought it was a good time to cash in." After thirteen years with the company, Wexler's priorities had inevitably shifted, but he still relished his early period at Atlantic. At the same time as he sought to sell the label, he tried to re-create the excitement of his early days with the company by looking for new artists whom audiences would turn to for a kind of emotional guidance.

Wexler's feet-first initiation into the business had been a trial-by-fire scenario. Along with Ertegun, he immediately took up the practice of writing songs himself, the most cost-effective way for the company to provide its artists with new material. It was tough sledding at first, considering Jerry was unfamiliar with how to count musical measures until engineering whiz Tom Dowd—one of the true visionaries of recorded music and perhaps Atlantic Records' shrewdest hire—taught him how. Still, his own compositional contributions helped yield "Soul on Fire" for LaVern Baker and "Warm Your Heart" for Clyde McPhatter. As Jerry himself recalls, "Those first couple of years at Atlantic had me flying high."

"We were having an absolutely fantastic success at Atlantic," Wexler told me. "We were a little Tiffany, nothing but hits and a fabulous roster. And we always put a great emphasis on bel canto. We liked people who could sing: Solomon Burke, Wilson Pickett, Ray Charles, Aretha Franklin. Our competitors didn't give a shit if they could sing or not. Somebody would walk in with a hit song— come on in, we'll cut it. One-off. We would take a song and save it. We had success with Aretha Franklin, because we knew how to record Ruth Brown and LaVern Baker—with the right musicians in the right context. We knew where the funk was, we knew where the bottom was." How did they know? "The answer is two words: Go figure."

The more successful the label got, however, the more neurotic and short-tempered Jerry became. His first wife, Shirley, tensed at the simple prospect of her husband's return home at the end of the day. The business consumed him, and over the course of a dozen years, Jerry became ever more obsessive and temperamental. Like the good Jewish boy he was, he worried, and in 1966 he was focused less on spending time in the studio than on convincing his partners to unload Atlantic. The company, he writes in his autobiography, *Rhythm and the Blues,* "was trying to recover from the double whammy of losing Ray Charles [to ABC Records] and Bobby Darin [to Capitol]. Together they had accounted for at least a third of our business."

Brother Ray had jumped ship in 1960, lured away by a more lucrative deal, and Wexler took his departure hard. He revered Ray Charles, dazzled not only by his virtuoso pianism and soulful vocal interpretive gifts, but by his sheer professionalism and forward-looking producing skills in the studio. Solomon Burke, the larger-than-life "King of Rock and Soul," was signed to the label, where he had significant success, but he couldn't replace Ray Charles.

Neither could the powerful and volatile Wilson Pickett, despite a number of classic hits. Early in his career, Wexler had been blessed to work with one of the geniuses of American music, the man who had virtually invented soul music by marrying gospel and blues. Pickett and "Mustang Sally" were certainly a boon to the company, but without a bona fide genius like Charles on the roster, Atlantic could surely only be seen as losing steam.

In the midst of contending with these pressures, Wexler had discovered, in late 1965, a little southern studio in Muscle Shoals, a small town in northwest Alabama, with a killer house band of fiercely funky white guys. Nearby Nashville and Memphis were the major centers of Southern musicianship, but somehow, impossibly, a vibrant music scene had been developing as well in the Alabama region known as the Shoals. Wexler fell in love with the laid-back vibe and quickly developed close and lasting relationships with the musicians, who, though hailing from an entirely different (Southern) orbit from Wex's Bronx-area beginnings, shared the exec's love of any music with a propulsive bottom end to it. Wexler quickly relocated Pickett's musical base of operations from Memphis to Muscle Shoals, where Wex found himself regularly commuting from his recently purchased home in Great Neck. (Ultimately, Wexler would become a kind of honorary Southerner: "I've learned Southern real good," he told me. "Did you know a lot of Southern boys call their close friends 'Honey'? And a lot of Southern boys, say, at the prep-school level, call 'pussy' 'cock.' I could use some good cock tonight. I spent so much time in the South. . . .")

Still, Wexler was distracted. How much was Atlantic Records worth? Would Ahmet agree to be divested of his brainchild and baby? And if so, who was likely to make an offer? These were the thoughts that consumed the window-washer's son—the man who in mid-1966 had a wife and three children to provide for, the self-described "fuck-up" for whom financial freedom had seemed utterly elusive—as he distractedly supervised Pickett's sessions in Muscle Shoals, berating himself for allowing eventual superstar Otis Redding to record on Atlantic subsidiary Stax rather than on Atlantic proper. Atlantic had given him every-thing, but he wasn't sure he could give Atlantic much more. An era—the Ray Charles era—seemed to be wind-ing down. How was Wex to know that another musical ge-nius would shortly alight on that remote Alabama town, deliver Atlantic its first ubiquitous million-selling hit since Sonny and Cher's "I Got You Babe," and increase expo-nentially the value of the company?

*J*ohn Hammond was relieved to see Aretha go. Six years had gone by since the producer had signed her to Colum-bia Records, securing her against a competing offer from

RCA and overseeing her first nongospel recordings. It wasn't that he had tired of working as her producer; in fact, he'd been only peripherally involved in the singer's career for the past few years. The Columbia powers that be (specifically, aristocratic chairman Goddard Lieberson and ambitious A&R man Dave Kapralik) had broken the news to Hammond upon his return from a vacation to Europe with his wife, Esmé, that Aretha Franklin, the woman he had signed to the label in 1960, whose rudimentary demo tape had convinced him that hers was "the most dynamic jazz voice [he'd] heard since Billie Holiday," was no longer his artist. He'd long ago accepted this decision, and contented himself with observing from the sidelines as a series of new producers smothered Aretha's gift under a phalanx of lush strings and encouraged her to sing show tunes meant to position her as what one observer has called "the black Barbra Streisand." It was this heartbreaking "musical misuse" that convinced Hammond that his find, whose Columbia contract in mid-1966 was on the verge of expiring, would be better off elsewhere.

Aretha was hardly the first supremely gifted, black woman singer Hammond had worked with. More than thirty years earlier he had drawn legendary blues woman Bessie Smith out of semiretirement, and he had gone to bat for her to insure she'd be properly compensated at a time when blues records weren't selling and Bessie's particular star was seen to have waned. A twenty-two-year-old Hammond had applied all his entrepreneurial moxie to the Smith project: convincing an intoxicated Bessie to agree to the session in a Philadelphia speakeasy; gathering, by sheer force of his own enthusiasm, a crew of master musicians, including "the king of blues trombone," Jack Teagarden, and the embodiment of swing, clarinetist Benny Goodman, to play on the record; paying for Smith's transit to New York with his own money; and somehow corralling the Empress of the Blues to the studio at the ungodly hour of 10:30 A.M.

This kind of instinct for putting artists together, for determining and establishing the necessary conditions for bringing about the making of music, was typical of Hammond, particularly when it came to jazz. Like his music-biz colleague (and quasi-protégé) Jerry Wexler, John Hammond was a lifelong devotee of all forms of black American music, having first fallen in love with the blues as a twelve-year-old who routinely blew his weekly one-dollar allowance on the records of artists whom he didn't even realize at the time weren't white. Hammond's parallels with Wexler are striking: both white men enraptured from a young age by black music; both record producers who started their music-industry careers as journalists; both involved in the early records of Aretha Franklin and Bob Dylan.

But if Wexler's passion for music widely associated with a black underclass made some surface sense owing to his quasi-outsider status as a second-generation Jewish immigrant, Hammond's zeal is harder to trace. Whereas Wexler was the quintessential tough kid from the Heights, John Hammond, the blues-lover who would let no hooch house deter him from listening to the musicians he admired, was a Vanderbilt. He grew up in New York City in a mansion on Fifth Avenue and Ninety-first Street, was educated at Hotchkiss, and was groomed from an early age to follow his father into a financially superfluous job in the law. His mother, the Bible-quoting Emily Vanderbilt Sloane Hammond, an activist by nature and beholden to a strictly enforced (and largely self-imposed) moral code that led her to do many good works on behalf of the poor, was, nevertheless, decidedly out of touch with the plight of black Americans in the early twentieth century. "Racial minorities were beyond her reach," Hammond wrote in his autobiography. "Blacks were porters and laundresses."

For young John, racial minorities were not only *within* his reach, they formed the core of his imaginative and artistic life. While his mother's obliviousness to racial strife was not inherited, her occasionally strident passion for restoring social order to an imbalanced world was. For his entire adult life, Hammond never left the house without the latest issue of *The Daily Worker, The New Republic,* or *New Masses* tucked under his arm. For a time he was employed by *The Nation*, for whom he reported on the notorious Scottsboro Boys case, in which two white Alabama women falsely accused nine black teenagers of gang rape. As early as the late 1920s he was a vocal supporter of the increasingly influential NAACP. Race played an almost inexplicably prominent role in the life of the self-described "reformer, certain in the right . . . an inheritor of the guilt and therefore the obligations of wealth." Indeed, it's impossible not to view, to some extent, what would become his crusade to further the careers of black artists as a way to expiate that guilt.

And yet, the psychology is almost irrelevant. With the "From Spirituals to Swing" concert, which he organized and which triumphed at Carnegie Hall in December 1938, Hammond's commitment to black artists was made unassailable. The performance brought together top black musicians across genres—including Count Basie, Lester Young, Sister Rosetta Tharpe, Charlie Christian, and a slew of other important artists—and presented them to an integrated audience. The aim was to educate white listeners and to promote African American musical traditions as worthy of being heard in a hall of Carnegie's stature. And it was done out of sheer love for the music. In his early sixties, Hammond commented on his relationship to black music: "One reason I'm the way I am is that I got to know

Harlem. Upper-class white folks went up to Harlem in the twenties slumming. I went out of passion. Anyone who did that had his life changed." With his own life altered, Hammond set about altering those of the musicians he admired. He resurrected (and virtually apotheosized) Bessie Smith and, what is even more significant, signed a nineteen-year-old Billie Holiday to her first recording contract.

Hammond first heard Billie at Monette Moore's bar-cum-jazz club in Harlem. Monette herself was the customary headliner, but when she was indisposed or out of town, the seen-it-all teen Holiday would fill in. He'd already produced Bessie and Benny, two titans of jazz, but for Hammond, Billie was a revelation. Her vocal instrument was meager from a range and power standpoint, but her ability to create intimacy, to weave her voice into a larger musical arrangement, and the sheer uniqueness of her sound were qualities Hammond had scarcely ever encountered before. He caught her show night after night, and was struck by how she would take the same songs and seemingly reinvent them from one performance to the next. He quickly made a convert of his future brother-in-law, Benny Goodman, who decided he needed to record with the singer. That was all the endorsement Columbia management needed (they did Benny's bidding much more quickly than they did John's), and Billie was brought in to lay down "Riffin' the Scotch" and "Your Mother's

Son-in-Law," a pair of silly songs characteristically elevated by Holiday's exuberant yet lacerating artistry.

Routine forays from Fifth Avenue to Harlem had introduced Hammond to Holiday. "Discovering" Aretha Franklin had been even simpler: Her demo simply showed up on his desk one day in 1960. It was handed off to him by composer Curtis Lewis as a songwriting showcase because it included his number "Today I Sing the Blues," cowritten with jazz singer Helen Humes, one of Hammond's favorite vocalists. If Hammond had already been intrigued, piqued, by the arrival of the rudimentary recording, he was stunned when he heard what came out— namely, the voice of eighteen-year-old Aretha Franklin. She instantly evoked for him a comparison with Holiday, that other onetime teenage phenom whose very being, in a similarly uncanny way, seemed to embody the kind of life experience that only listeners four times her age could have felt. Is there any more emotionally powerful force than the voice, especially one at once youthful and wise, one of a unique timbral cast, one simultaneously appealing to the ear and evocative of a kind of universal, profoundly human subtext? That's what Billie did to John, with her unaccountable ability to bring him to tears, and that's what the demo from this daughter of a well-known preacher was doing as well.

At the time, Aretha was under the tutelage of her soon-to-be manager Jo King, to whose West Side recording studio Hammond promptly repaired to hear the young gospel dynamo in the flesh. He offered her a deal, and Aretha and her father, their hearts set on forming an alliance with a major, international, well-respected label, eagerly accepted.

They had gone into the studio almost immediately; years later Hammond would call that first session "one of the three or four most exciting in my life in recording." Aretha's performance of "Today I Sing the Blues," the Curtis Lewis song of her demo, was the first song recorded: "I sometimes wonder if she ever made a better record," Hammond wrote. Some of these early tracks had been truly great (in addition to "Today I Sing the Blues," "Won't Be Long," "(Blue) By Myself" and "Maybe I'm a Fool" stand out); none had been less than vocally mesmerizing. Aretha's then-self-titled debut is now reissued as *The Great Aretha Franklin: The First 12 Sides*, and Hammond, to be sure, had been generally thrilled with these first recordings. His instincts regarding Aretha's talent and promise were utterly satisfied by her first forays into professional recording.

But that was six years earlier, and things had changed. Not with Aretha—her gift was untarnished and as full of vibrancy as it had ever been. But John had essentially been left out in the cold. It no longer mattered what he thought was the best way to unveil Aretha's still-concealed power.

In his own words, Hammond was "greatly disturbed" by the rather static nontrajectory of Aretha's Columbia stint, but his faith in her ability never wavered. "She had every musicianly quality I thought she had," he wrote. "All she needed was to hold to her roots in the church." The man so instrumental in the deification of Bessie Smith and Billie Holiday had similarly anointed Aretha Franklin, had placed her along the popular-music continuum with those legendary forebears as their musical legatee, though she had yet to fully substantiate his lavish claims on her behalf. Surely *someone*, some label, some producer would be able to tap into Aretha's genius to an extent that Columbia, despite its significant output with the singer, had not. Everyone who had worked with her—Hammond, Bryant, producers Clyde Otis and Robert Mersey—had been instantly clued in to Aretha's talent, but a formula for harnessing that talent remained elusive. Aretha was lost to John Hammond, and that was the best thing for Aretha.

Rick Hall had his sights set on the big leagues. He'd been a fixture in the northwest Alabama music scene for fifteen years, and though singing and playing lead guitar for the Fairlanes in the fifties hadn't exactly made him a household name outside the nucleus of Colbert County towns where they most often gigged, Hall knew he had talent, and, better still, he had a studio. Fame, or Florence Alabama

Musical Enterprises, was originally a music publishing company and recording studio conceived in 1959 by Tom Stafford, a local Florence character viewed in town as something of an oracle for his seemingly uncanny grasp of a music business that had yet to invade the Florence–Muscle Shoals–Tuscumbia axis. Rick had been an early partner in the venture, but when the relationship soured (largely because of what most agree to be Hall's often bull-headed approach to interpersonal relationships), he was ousted with only the company name to console him. That was in 1960; two years later, Hall established the new Fame in nearby Muscle Shoals, just across the Tennessee River from Florence. He began working as a salesman for a used-car dealer, married the man's daughter, and got his father-in-law's help in building the first Muscle Shoals incarnation of Fame Studios in a former tobacco warehouse. A local singer named Arthur Alexander came to Fame, and Rick produced his song "You Better Move On." Alexander was gospel-trained, but "You Better Move On" was an early country-soul hybrid. The song almost inexplicably became a top-forty hit, and the Muscle Shoals music scene was officially up and rolling. It wasn't long after that, that Fame was ready to present its loose, airy, heavy country funk to a larger audience, and Rick's recently inaugurated association with Atlantic's Jerry Wexler looked like the means to do just that.

Almost four decades later, Hall remembers vividly the brief but potent flame-up that was his relationship with Wexler, and readily points out that it was the Atlantic exec who helped put Fame, and Muscle Shoals, on the map. "My friend Joe Galkin called Jerry and said, 'I've got this young man, Rick Hall. He's gonna be a comer,'" Rick drawls, Alabama-style. Galkin was a New York record promoter who'd unaccountably become convinced that the South was the place to be, musically speaking, and who'd quickly become a fixture in the Atlanta, Memphis, and Alabama music scenes. Rick Hall, in Muscle Shoals, was one of his Southern finds.

"Joe put me on the phone," Rick continues, "and Jerry said, 'If you run into something that you think might be a hit, send it my way and let's make some money.' About a month later, I called him and said I had something. He said, 'Rick, it's a Sunday. I'm with my family, we're out swimming. Can it wait?' And I said, 'This is a hit. You said, Call me when you've got a hit.' So I sent it. He got it. And he called me and said, 'Are you sure this is a hit? I don't know, Rick . . . ' He tried to put me off. I said, 'It's a *big* hit, Jerry. Trust me.'"

Wexler doesn't recall being quite as uncertain of the song's potential as Hall describes, but Rick and Jerry often remember events differently, a divergence of the minds that would present itself, confusingly, as I spoke to both men about the Aretha sessions in Muscle Shoals. Either way, the song Hall was pushing on Wex was "When a Man Loves a Woman," by Percy Sledge, and it became a number-one hit for Atlantic in the summer of 1966. "And the rest is history," Hall says.

Wex had established ties to the South even earlier, recognizing that, away from New York, there existed the opportunity to cut funky records relatively inexpensively. Several years earlier he'd orchestrated a production-and-distribution deal with the legendary soul label Stax Records, in Memphis. But Muscle Shoals and Rick Hall were different. Jerry both liked and was put off by the swaggering chieftain of Fame. "I was the young whippersnapper, full of piss and vinegar," Hall acknowledges today, though the expression is perhaps something of an understatement as it applies to him. Even in his early thirties, he was a "souped-up salesman and hard-nosed entrepreneur," as Wexler calls him. Indeed, Rick was nothing if not ambitious, and he had the requisite country-boy chutzpah to believe that out-of-the-way Muscle Shoals could become a musical power.

Rick knew that a link to Atlantic Records was vital to Fame's success, but he was dubious of Wex's skills as a producer. "Don't get me wrong," Hall told me. "I love Jerry Wexler. I think he's the greatest record executive who ever walked on two legs. But we didn't think of him as a producer."

But regardless of Wex's musical background, Rick acknowledges that "Jerry was the best teacher I ever had," and that his apprenticeship, as it were, would prove to be mutually beneficial. "When a Man Loves a Woman" made a small fortune for Atlantic, and in return the label had bestowed on Hall the electric Wilson Pickett, with whom he cut "Land of 1,000 Dances" and "Funky Broadway." Both Wexler and Hall were headstrong, willful, opinionated personalities (they still are), and their relationship, even at this early and fruitful stage, was not without its moments of abrasiveness, of discontent. But hell, so far, so good, each thought. Wexler was getting hits for the company and Hall was making a name for himself. Pickett's "Mustang Sally" was in the can. Rick wondered which artist Jerry would bring down next.

*A*retha Franklin doesn't once mention Rick Hall in her 1999 autobiography, but as one of the architects of a brand of soul that both Jerry Wexler (directly) and John Hammond (indirectly) felt would be the means for Aretha to unleash her unprecedented talent onto the world, his role in her musical arrival is undeniable. A brash Jew from the Bronx, a lock-jaw old-money heir, and a southern country boy from Alabama—these were the figures who, from a professional standpoint, helped a young girl in her twenties from Detroit, a mother since her teens who hadn't completed high school, become the embodiment of black womanhood. She was the first lady in the funk collective Parliament/Funkadelic's whimsical concept of a utopian "Chocolate City" (Muhammad Ali was the president), and the greatest soul singer in the world. No one had a greater influence on Aretha than her father, and the fact that she learned and refined her art in the gospel church is inarguable. It's ironic that, though the Reverend C. L. Franklin sired Aretha, and her talent came straight out of the black musical tradition, three white men helped birth the Queen of Soul.

three

The Jazz Singer

*A*retha Franklin missed her kids. She'd spent the past six years, ever since signing with Columbia Records in 1960 and embarking on her secular career, shuttling back and forth between New York City and her hometown of Detroit. Her sons, nine-year-old Clarence (born when Aretha was fourteen), seven-year-old Eddie, and baby Teddy, though with her now, had spent a lot of time back home on LaSalle Boulevard in the care of the singer's father and grandmother, known to all as Big Mama. For much of the time, Aretha's base of operations had been, inevitably, New York, the only option for a jazz singer hoping to have hits and gig regularly. She visited home as often as she could, and had been able to purchase a place on Detroit's Fourteenth Street, thus creating a Michigan home base that made her separations from the boys a little less agonizing. Over time she became somewhat accustomed to lengthy absences (balanced by the occasionally lengthy visit) from her kids, and she knew that Big Mama would keep a loving and watchful eye over them. Still, it nagged at her. Aretha knew firsthand what it was like to grow up with a largely absent mother.

Barbara Siggers Franklin, Aretha's mother, herself an accomplished gospel singer and pianist, died when Aretha was ten years old, though she had in fact relinquished the day-to-day duties of mothering even earlier. When Aretha was six, Barbara had separated abruptly (or so it seemed to her young children) from her husband and moved back to her hometown of Buffalo, New York, taking her eldest child, Vaughn, with her. Aretha and her other siblings, Cecil, Erma, and Carolyn, were reared by their father and paternal grandmother, the same pair caring, off and on, for Aretha's own kids in the midsixties.

Barbara's flight from her family remains, even today, a touchy subject for Aretha. Over the years it has been reported that Siggers "abandoned" her family, a charge Aretha vehemently denies, citing her and her siblings' extended annual summer visits to Buffalo as proof of her mother's devotion. To this day she maintains long-standing feuds with Gladys Knight and Cissy Houston (her onetime backup singer), not over vocal supremacy, but because of the singers' outspokenness on the question of Aretha's mother's alleged desertion.

Aretha's steadfast refusal to admit that there was anything unusual, or frankly devastating, in her mother's relocation is hard to understand. Why can't the singer concede that having her mother present one day and gone the next might have been painful for her? Where would be the shame in talking about what it was like, as a youngster, to suddenly find herself bereft of a parent? Not to mention how that loss affected her art, which surely it did. In her autobiography, *From These Roots*, published in 1999, Aretha issued a relatively terse statement. "In no way, shape, form, or fashion did our mother desert us. She was extremely responsible, loving, and caring," Aretha says—but not much else. Whatever the reasons for her reticence, her virtual silence on the subject is representative of a constant in Aretha's life, an unwillingness to offer up for public consumption topics of a personal nature. "She's a private person," Aretha's ex-husband and former manager Ted White told me. "She just feels like, Hey, my inward self is my business. I'm not public in that respect. Buy my records if you want my music."

"She kind of idealizes everything," explains David Ritz, the coauthor of Franklin's autobiography. "She pulls down the shade. She's hit the delete button. I think she's really private, and I think she hasn't processed a lot of stuff. And if you don't process it, you don't want to publicize it, because you don't know exactly what *it* is."

Aretha's silence is commendable on the one hand and unsatisfying on the other. The question of her oft-declared (though not by her) inner anguish has been overstated in many accounts, resulting in a portrait of the singer as dogged by tragedy and tormented by unnamable sorrows. ("Please be careful," Wexler warned, protectively, of writing about Aretha. "She's very sensitive.") But the fact that she endured some personal emotional hardship is hard to argue against ("She's had her problems," her beloved younger sister Carolyn said). Two teen pregnancies, her mother's flight, difficulties in her personal relationships, her ongoing struggle with her weight, her father's 1979 shooting and subsequent death, sister Carolyn's and brother Cecil's deaths from cancer, the fact that, today, Aretha remains the last of her siblings still living—these are not insignificant woes for anyone to endure. "The blues people live on tragedy," says Nikki Giovanni, a friend of Franklin's and the author of the chill-inducing "Poem for Aretha," written in 1968, which portrays the singer as an ordinary woman with problems, just like the rest of us, but whose problems are elevated, crystallized, imbued with extra gravitas by her art and thrown into relief by her status as a star. "The blues people have pain. Without pain, you'd have to go sing rock-and-roll! Pain is part of anybody's life, and I think Aretha has handled it as well as anybody. She expresses it in her music. Like Faith Ringgold expresses it in her quilts."

Depictions of Aretha as victimized, in pain, and weak generally annoy the singer; it's as if she can't bear her lack of control over what is said of her. But, whether she is truly "our lady of mysterious sorrows," as Jerry Wexler described her, or simply a woman who's withstood some significantly hard knocks (as I believe), the fact is that Aretha does not discuss whatever demons she may have; whatever she's feeling comes out in her songs.

The near silence regarding her mother's departure is probably an issue of personal pride: In the fifties and sixties the Franklins were virtual royalty in Detroit, and royalty seldom admits to anything less than a pristine family life. Aretha Franklin, despite her superstar status, is family-oriented and finds any blight on her family's name to be excruciating. Moreover, it can't have been lost on the singer that there were certain almost eerie parallels in the reality that her own kids, for long stretches, were under the primary guidance of C. L. and Big Mama rather than their mother, just as she, as a child, had been under the primary guidance of C. L. and Big Mama rather than her own mother.

C. L. Franklin was certainly enough of an outsize personality to serve as both parents at once. If the prodigiously talented child Aretha, adept from a young age not only as a singer but on the piano as well, was something of a local celebrity, her father was a central national figure in the black church. Aretha inherited much of her mother's vocal ability; she got her intensity, passion, and charisma from her father. Jesse Jackson, a close Franklin family friend, called C. L. "the high priest of soul preaching . . . a combination of soul and science and substance and sweetness." It's a complex mixture born of hard times endured and promise fulfilled through hard work and faith. But the description doesn't even begin to capture the magnitude of C. L.'s magnetism, the profound power he held over his congregation, associates, friends, and family, most notably his talented daughter, whose genius he recognized early. Aretha's childhood musical debut at New Bethel Baptist Church, her teenage gospel recording there, the demo she shopped to Columbia when she'd made the decision to pursue crossing over to the pop world, were all carefully, even scrupulously, superintended by C. L. The reverend is routinely called a "soul preacher," but in a sense he was more of a pop preacher, committed to his spiritual work but willing, even eager, to make money and achieve renown, aims he passed onto Aretha.

Clarence LaVaughn Franklin was born in 1915 in Mississippi, and as a young boy his father left the family, never to return, an uncanny precursor to Aretha's childhood maternal loss. The boy's mother, Rachel (the name "Big Mama" would come later), soon remarried, and C. L. and his sister Louise were lovingly reared by their step-father, Henry Franklin, a sharecropper whose surname they adopted. Rachel and Henry would have another child, Aretha, for whom the future Queen of Soul would be named. Aretha's other aunt provided the singer's middle name, Louise.

As a boy, C. L. was less than enthralled with his family's farming lifestyle; what he was drawn to was school and the church, which his mother attended each week without fail. At about age twelve, bookish yet popular C. L. had a spiritual awakening that convinced him that "I was called to preach." In his teens he left home to embark on the life of the traveling preacher, delivering sermons in Kentucky, Michigan, and Arkansas and around his home state of Mississippi. Soon after, he met Aretha's mother, Barbara, whom he first glimpsed singing and playing piano in a Shelby, Mississippi, church. The couple soon started having children, moved to Memphis, Tennessee (where Aretha was born, on March 25, 1942), before ultimately settling in Detroit. There C. L.'s reputation was made at the New Bethel Baptist Church, as was a substantial living, thanks to regular radio broadcasts and recordings of his increasingly popular sermons.

Franklin had a kind, open face, a powerful charisma, and

a stirring speaking voice that commanded attention. He was a musical preacher, a natural singer whose delivery, when he was particularly inspired, straddled the line of the spoken and the sung. The "whooping" style of Baptist and Pentecostal ministry was not unique to Reverend Franklin, but he was one of its most gifted and imitated practitioners. His delivery could get so intense, could rise to such a fever pitch, that attendants were employed in his church to minister to overcome parishioners who routinely fainted in the aisles. Church attendees got happy when C. L. preached, speaking in tongues, traipsing up and down the aisles, shrieking, collapsing, feeling the spirit. The fifties, the decade during which Aretha cut her gospel teeth and C. L.'s popularity soared, was a high point in the history of gospel. It was a period when singers like Mahalia Jackson were garnering international reputations, and Reverend Franklin was a Baptist-gospel world leader. "The Man with the Million-Dollar Voice," as he came to be known, delivered radio-broadcast sermons that might rake in as much as five thousand dollars, a hefty sum in the mid-1950s. He was not just a friend to Martin Luther King, Jr., a fact for which he would be widely and affectionately remembered, he was also a major influence on King's preaching style.

But Reverend Franklin was no demure man of the cloth, and his gospel-circuit celebrity made him a fixture in a circle otherwise populated by musicians and performers. He was an upstanding symbol of racial pride and religious authority, who, nonetheless, was busted for marijuana in 1969 and who was forced to pay a considerable fine for tax evasion years after that. "He was a very liberal minister," Carolyn Franklin said. "Which kept us in trouble, because he knew all the performers in both realms: pop and gospel. And in the fifties, it was unusual for a minister to have that kind of association outside the church." Still, as Jesse Jackson points out, "C. L. Franklin was rare, not just unique; famous because he was well known, but great because of his service," service that can't be forgotten in the light of his occasional legal trouble. (As Aretha herself says, "Daddy was a minister, and he was also a man.") Reverend Franklin might deliver an impassioned, moralistic sermon on a given morning and keep the neighbors up that night, with house parties attended by Sam Cooke, Dinah Washington, Lionel Hampton, Art Tatum, and other music-world luminaries.

It was at these starry gatherings that Aretha's gift first shone beyond her family circle. Tatum might be called on to do a number on the household piano; perhaps there would be a song performed on the spot by Nat "King" Cole. Next on the program would be a preteen Aretha, summoned from her room upstairs by her father. It must have been simultaneously daunting and exhilarating for young Ree, a child called upon to perform, at odd hours, for an audience of grown-ups, masters in music waiting to be impressed by the little girl C. L. had boasted of. These weren't audiences of adoring aunts and uncles; this was, Sing for Nat. Play for Art. In her autobiography, Aretha paints herself as somewhat beleaguered by her father's household performance requests, but surely she was terrified as well. Of course, it didn't take more than a few late-night living room triumphs for the girl to develop a sure sense of her talent and the effect it could have on people, even famous musicians. "He would drag her out of bed," Aretha's sister Erma recalled, referring to their father. "And she'd go down there and play for the stars. And they considered *her* a star once they heard her."

If her impromptu performances for famous family friends gave Aretha some confidence in her musical gifts, touring with Daddy's gospel caravan as a teenager gave her much-needed experience and stage chops. In the late fifties, Reverend Franklin toured extensively throughout the Midwest and the Northeast, delivering sermons like "The Eagle Stirreth Her Nest" and "The Prodigal Son" to adoring throngs and employing his talented daughter (whom he paid fifty dollars per show) as his opening act. An absurdly precocious Aretha had already cut a gospel album at age fourteen (around the same time she had her first child), recorded live at her father's church and now famous for the prophetic cry of "Listen at her! Listen at her!" by an overwhelmed listener in the congregation. On tour with her father, she grew close with some of the gospel artists she admired and learned from.

In 1966, however, at age twenty-four, Aretha Franklin was churning out sides for Columbia and garnering little acclaim for her efforts. She missed those gospel tours, longed for the camaraderie of the other artists, and longed for Daddy to be around. But after having traveled for several years with the show, she had decided, at age eighteen, that she wanted to sing secular music. She had observed closely as Sam Cooke made his wildly successful plunge from the church to the pop charts and decided that she would try the same. Showing considerable moxie she told her father of her plan. "I decided I wanted to change fields," she recalled in 1967, shortly after *I Never Loved a Man* hit. "So I let him know, and he felt that this is what I wanted to do and what I should do." Indeed, it's striking that, even as a teenage daddy's girl, a quiet creature who spent most of her time, when she wasn't performing, at the Arcadia roller-skating rink in central Detroit, Aretha somehow had the confidence not to ask her father's permission, but to *inform* him that she had made certain artistic decisions that necessitated, if not a severing, at least a loosening of her ties to the church that had nurtured her for her entire life. "Shy," "withdrawn" Aretha was nevertheless a young woman in ever-growing command of her musical gifts, and she had a definite idea of how she wanted to put them to use. The Reverend was supportive of her choice to "go pop" and had helped her produce and shop a demo, hooking her up with the talented bass player Major Holly, a Detroiter who did session work in New York, to oversee the project. But the ultimate decision about what route to take had been hers, and she had never regretted it.

That said, the instant triumph she had to some degree anticipated at Columbia had yet to pan out. And outside the studio, away from the microphone, things weren't all right in Aretha's life. Her marriage to the volatile Ted White was increasingly strained. Daddy hated him. "His motivation is not sincere," her father had said of Ted. This was especially hard to take, because, in Aretha's world, no one was more important than Daddy. Aretha was accustomed to finding sanctuary in her singing, relief from her personal travails, but somehow performing tepid numbers like "Misty" and "Over the Rainbow," as much as she loved those songs, wasn't really singing—not like tearing through "Precious Lord, Take My Hand" or "How I Got Over" in front of an impassioned congregation. *That* was the kind of musical immersion that could help the singer forget, albeit temporarily, the troubles with Ted, the struggle of being a twenty-four-year-old woman with nine-year-old and seven-year-old sons and an infant, the sense of being adrift at having no mother of her own to help guide her. The worry that she wasn't a sufficiently attentive mother was particularly vexing.

But what was she to do? There was The Voice to contend with. And just as her children had needs, so did Aretha, herself little more than a child, and so did her voice, a virtual entity unto itself whose need to flourish would not be denied, nor would Aretha ever deign to. As longtime Aretha observer Gerri Hirshey writes in her valuable survey *Nowhere to Run: The Story of Soul Music*, "Aretha said that singing had taken her places she couldn't get to any other way—to a zone where she was so much herself that none of us would recognize her." The knowledge that she could access that zone virtually at will was a facet of Aretha's personality both empowering and impossible to ignore. *Real* life seemed to unfold while she was singing, immersed in music. As a result, certain quotidian details were bound to fall by the wayside.

A twenty-four-year-old trying to build on the slight foothold she had in the music industry, hoping to unfurl her gift, that fact of herself that *was* most herself, the personal characteristic by which she'd always been known to everyone as well as to herself—Reverend Franklin's daughter, the one with the voice—has her hands full when, in the midst of everything the business is throwing at her, she has to endure the anguish of knowing her kids might be several states away, the frustration of not yet having had the hits that somehow felt like a birthright, and the anxiety of being married to a mercurial man who also happened to be her manager. At least by then she and Ted had a Manhattan apartment. At least there was comfort in the knowledge that there was a man around to take care of her, to return home to, to cook for, to kibbitz with about that day's activity at the studio or that evening's gig at the Village Vanguard or the Copacabana. It was certainly an improvement over a few years earlier, when Clarence and Eddie were back home in Detroit and Aretha was holed up in the YWCA, nervous about living in the Big Apple, lonely, and without the comforting, galvanizing presence of Daddy.

Being married, though not without its difficulties, was something of a relief. While husband Ted didn't necessarily share the conviction of Columbia brass that to move on from the tradition-minded, small-combo jazz orientation of her first, John Hammond–produced records in favor of lush balladry would bring hits, at least she could leave that aspect of her career to him. She appreciated Hammond for his respect for gospel, not to mention for the fact that he initially sent her into the studio with the lavishly talented gospel and jazz pianist Ray Bryant chiefly because of their shared Baptist background. She hadn't done much damage on the charts with those first singles, except for "Rock-A-Bye Your Baby with a Dixie Melody," which managed to break the top forty, but they were songs she loved, and she'd been excited about her foray into a realm outside gospel. "This material was close to my heart," she would later tell David Ritz. "Until then I was singing gospel, so this was my first time out with so-called standards. I was excited, and pleased, that it was coming off so well." "She digs Columbia!" Ritz told me, recreating the period. "She doesn't mind wanting to be the next Diahann Carroll. If it had happened, it would have happened, and I think homegirl would have loved it! It just didn't happen. So it isn't that they had a gun to her head and told her, Do this, do that. I think she was happy. It's just that she didn't have any hits." If management thought that a few production alterations would bring sales success, well, she was all for it. She wasn't convinced that this was the right route, but she would leave strategy to the others; the singing, the time spent in front of the mic—that was her area. Let Ted devise a sales scheme; she would deliver, vocally, whatever was asked of her.

What they'd lately been asking of her were ballads. It was the latest in a sequence of unfocused shifts in genre that had established Aretha, among critics and DJs, as a singer capable of virtually anything, but that had succeeded only in confusing the record-buying public. "I was having what were called 'turntable hits,'" Franklin told an interviewer years later. "Records that get a lot of play but did not garner a lot of sales. We wanted hits! Everyone else was having hits and I didn't have one hit record."

The hits were meant to have arrived with the 1964 release of the *Runnin' Out of Fools* album, Aretha's first foray into rhythm and blues after five LPs of jazzier material. In addition to the self-effacing yet funky title track, this album's highlights were an impassioned remake of Dionne Warwick's slicker "Walk On By" and what's surely the most soulful rendition of "The Shoop Shoop Song" ever to have been put on wax. But despite Aretha's ever-emotional presentation, this was nevertheless a brand of R&B far removed from the gut-wrenching, to-the-rafters soul that would make her reputation just a few years later. The abrupt shift in direction (*Runnin' Out of Fools*' predecessor was a Dinah Washington tribute album that featured the Nat Cole–identified "Unforgettable," the Washington signature "What a Diff'rence a Day Makes," and other jazz-pop fare not exactly known for tearing the roof off the sucker) failed to jolt fans into opening their wallets. Aretha began to wonder if she'd been mistaken to so wholly entrust career decisions to Columbia management and to Ted. But Columbia was an internationally recognized label, and in her own words, Aretha was pleased simply to be with a major company. "I was still naïve about the business of the music industry," she recalled. "I was happy to have the opportunity to sing and responded positively to the songs and producers who came my way. I was down for the music and missed the political nuances; I was in my own world of music."

Aretha's strong sense of pride and personal importance, inevitable for a daughter of the commanding C. L. Franklin, was satisfied by her association with an old-time company of Columbia's stature. But though she had no regrets about having signed with Hammond, she couldn't help but ponder what her career would have been like had she gone instead with a fledgling Detroit label that had also been eager, when Aretha was starting out, to add her to its roster.

In 1960, Motown had a mere handful of artists on the payroll. The now-iconic music mogul Berry Gordy was simply an intensely ambitious local boy who rightly sensed that his hometown of Detroit was a hotbed of as yet unheralded talent. Smokey Robinson (best friend to Aretha's brother Cecil), Mary Wilson, Diane Ross ("Diana" would come later), and Mary Wells were all talented local teens who would benefit beyond reason from Gordy's show-business acumen. And though his conviction that the gawky, thin-voiced Diane Ross had it in her to become a superstar may have required vision, the notion that Aretha was destined for greatness was a no-brainer. In the late fifties Gordy and then-partner Billy Davis courted Aretha, came to her father's house, and played their songs on the family piano to try and lure her to their still-forming label. But the Franklin pride (and C. L.'s wishes) prohibited the family's most talented member from signing over her career to an untested entity. By most accounts, Aretha's decision to pass on Motown was a wise or at least fortuitous one: Hitsville, U.S.A.'s formula for tailoring tepid "soul" music to a white, middle-class audience by means of a punishingly obvious downbeat that even the most rhythmically challenged Caucasian teen couldn't miss was utterly at odds with Franklin's improvisational and emotion-drenched musical sensibility. The unprecedented gospel-trained soul that even in 1960 had begun to burn and grow within Aretha Franklin would only have been stifled by the rigid production techniques employed at Motown.

"It was wonderful that Aretha did not sign with Motown, because she never would have been a hit at Motown," says Nikki Giovanni. She was a fan of Aretha since she heard the singer's original composition "Without the One You Love," recorded for Columbia Records, and a friend since shortly after the publication of her own verse tribute "Poem for Aretha." "She's not the Voice of Young America," Giovanni told me, referring to Motown's catchphrase. "She's the voice of old America. Aretha is the blues, is gospel, is down-home, is fried chicken, is chitlins. Aretha is, Put your feet up under the table. Aretha is, Don't worry about it, baby, it'll be alright. And that's *not* the Motown sound. She was very, very fortunate that C. L. understood that. I'm a fan of Berry Gordy's, but that would have been a disastrous, talent-killing relationship."

In 1966, Aretha was not yet regarded as fried chicken and chitlins, but she nonetheless knew that Motown was not for her. But, still hitless, she couldn't help but be a bit rankled by the impending world domination of the Supremes, a group of girls that Aretha knew firsthand weren't in possession of anything close to her ability. (She was, nevertheless, friendly with the girls, and when founding Supreme Flo Ballard died in 1976, C. L. Franklin presided over her funeral at New Bethel Baptist Church.) She never regretted, but she certainly wondered at the professional turn of events. If she had gone with another label, worked from the outset with a producer other than John Hammond, would she be the jazz singer she was today?

Aretha wasn't even sure that a "jazz singer" was in fact what she truly was. She had certainly been spending plenty of time singing numbers like "Lover, Come Back to Me" and "God Bless the Child" in jazz venues across the East Coast, but for some time she had been conscious of another musical identity forming inside her, a kind of alternate musical self that she hadn't been using. Hammond had loved the gospel fervor of her singing, but at

Columbia, a "white company," as Hammond himself described it, she'd had to rein in her deluxe vocalism.

Years later, Ahmet Ertegun not only deems Aretha a jazz singer but one of the best he's ever heard, and suggests that Hammond didn't do enough to nurture Franklin's jazz skills. "The thing with John Hammond was, he would drop things," Ertegun says today. "He would find someone and then lose interest. He was never really truly engaged as an employee by a record company. Is that what you call a dilettante? Now, I was asked recently who's my favorite jazz singer. And when you say 'jazz singer,' it's hard to tell what makes Ella Fitzgerald more of a jazz singer, say, than Peggy Lee. Actually, they're really pop singers. Billie Holiday just sang pop songs. Bessie Smith was much more of a jazz singer. Well, I said, I know a number who could be considered jazz singers. So I picked my favorite jazz singer, and that's Aretha Franklin. I love the way she sings straight songs. When she sings a song straight, there's a lot of jazz in it. Her voice has the kind of blues inflection that, when she does improvisation, she does no wrong. It just turns on."

What Aretha could do was certainly awe-inspiring to those who worked with her, but it was also a bit frightening, unwieldy from a marketing point of view. Was the average pop-music listener prepared for what Ted White referred to as Aretha's "raw power"? Pulling back was something she knew how to do, and was becoming accustomed to doing, but it wasn't a way of singing that presented her truest self to the world. Inside, there were large emotions itching to be released in a large and emotional way. What's more, Aretha had fragments of songs she'd started composing floating around in her head and taking shape. According to White, the couple had written a number of songs that they were hanging on to, waiting for the right circumstances to unveil them. In six years Columbia had released only four of Aretha's original songs. She'd wept the first time she walked into the studio and heard producer Robert Mersey's full-orchestra arrangements for her tune "Without the One You Love" (which, in fact, was more effective in a small-combo version recorded a few years later). But moments like that had been rare. "I am a very creative, artsy kind of person," Aretha told an interviewer, almost poignantly. But throughout the Columbia years, she had been much more a mere singer (albeit a fabulous one) than a multifaceted creative force.

Aretha wasn't the only one who sensed that her excessive potential remained untapped. The fact that she was, musically speaking, bursting at the seams was hard to ignore. Louise Williams Bishop, at the time a prominent Philadelphia DJ and friend of the Franklin family, as well as an instrumental force in the development of Aretha's career (she's now a Pennsylvania Democrat in the House of Representatives) told me, "I always felt that she was holding something back, and not really releasing everything she could release in those Columbia records." Bishop remembered Aretha from her teenage gospel days, was a fan of her first album, the gospel record, *Never Grow Old*, which Aretha had unleashed barely into her teens. "She was obviously with people who didn't really know gospel and didn't hear the gospel that was in 'Retha or the soul that was in 'Retha," Bishop continues. "She was to some degree *contained*. Knowing her as a gospel singer, I just felt something was missing. It wasn't all that was Aretha."

Clyde Otis, Aretha's producer on five Columbia LPs, agrees. "I knew that she wasn't going to make it at Columbia," Otis says today. "Columbia was into a groove that did not suit her. Period. I kept telling Ted White, You've got to let her express more. He said, I know, Clyde, but look, they don't *want* her to express more at Columbia." Aretha herself confided in Otis that she was dissatisfied. "She said, 'I'm so frustrated about this situation,'" the producer recalls. "'I don't know how to feel.'" Ted White, however, says that he and his talented wife didn't have the time to be particularly upset by any kind of slight from the label. "We had so many other things going on," he remembers. "We were just putting together a band, we'd just started to do top clubs throughout the country, and all that was exciting. So we just kind of relaxed and felt that if the record was going to come it was going to come."

In 1966, Aretha was an extraordinarily talented singer locked in a groove she wasn't feeling, a young woman with gospel glory in her voice and gospel lore surrounding her name. She was working like a dog, in the studio and on the club circuit, though great success eluded her. But she didn't panic. She never second-guessed her abilities. She simply showed up and continued to sing. Regardless of what record-label politics may have been swirling around her, Aretha, I believe, found solace, power even, in the sheer fact of her voice. As the time on her Columbia contract evaporated, Aretha went deeper into her music. How could she get worked up about business details? *She* was the one with the voice. The gift of a superb singing voice brings with it a tremendous power, an almost unshakable sense of self, immune to whatever personal or professional issues might surround one. So, although six years had gone by at Columbia during which time Aretha's records failed to seize the public's imagination as would her later work, she wasn't particularly distressed. When she walked into a room, Aretha was the one who could sing, and, at the time, at least, that was good enough for her.

"A change is gonna come," she must have thought, pondering her career as it neared a crossroads. Aside from the inchoate desire to be doing something different, something newer, something more expressive of her inner life, there were practical issues that were leading Franklin to a new mode of musical expression. The conclusion of her association with Columbia Records was nearing, and Ted White had secured an offer from Mercury Records that they were viewing as a backup. Aretha was writing songs and even contemplated recording herself. She *would* figure out a means to produce the music that was stirring inside of her. And if that didn't work out, she could always return to her father's church and the life of a gospel singer.

four

From the Church to the Charts

Gospel people generally don't take kindly to singers from their ranks making bids at pop stardom. It's seen as distasteful, irreligious, almost vulgarly ambitious. Even gospel legends like Sam Cooke and Sister Rosetta Tharpe were summarily rejected by the church community when, after achieving mainstream, popular success, they made well-intentioned attempts to return to the fold. Cooke in particular (Sam Cooke!), the man who, with "You Send Me," brought black pop to the top of the charts—endured the singular, and devastating, indignity of being utterly dismissed by a Chicago audience when he rejoined his legendary original gospel group, the Soul Stirrers, for an anniversary concert. And not much has changed in the forty years since then. "Gospel is big business," points out the reigning matriarch of sacred singing, Shirley Caesar, emphasizing that there's a good or even great living to be had for a gospel singer, in an urgent attempt to dissuade talented singers from making the often irreparable move of pursuing the pop charts.

She's right. Gospel *is* big business, and it's a business that enjoys the benefit of the authoritative stewardship of, well, the Lord. Gospel's ability to survive and thrive apart from the rest of the music world is extraordinary, and the genre is certainly worthy of the almost universal reverence it's afforded. That reverence derives from the thrilling, powerful voices of gospel, voices of virtually unprecedented character and virtuosity outside an operatic context. A great gospel singer "wrecks," "destroys," or "tears up" audiences (choose your own metaphor of decimation) by alternating, like a great opera singer, between unleashing glorious tones of overwhelming power at one moment and sacrificing tonal beauty for the sake of getting a feeling across most effectively the next.

In his landmark survey *The Gospel Sound,* Anthony Heilbut writes that church singing "simply reformed all our listening expectations," specifically citing (in a vivid musicological coinage) "Aretha Franklin's pyrotechnique." This revamped notion of just what one could expect from a vocalist, however, for a long time was largely restricted to Baptist and Pentecostal church-goers. The impassioned alto of Mahalia Jackson and the vocal pizzazz of Clara Ward had, of course, hit the airwaves already, and popular soul singers like LaVern Baker and Ruth Brown weren't without a churchy fervor. But though Mahalia was a national icon, it was Aretha, along with Ray Charles, who made the kind of heaven-and-earth singing at which she excelled palpable to a mass audience tuned in primarily to mainstream radio. "Gospel has its own very superior aesthetic standards," Heilbut continues. "The audience's musical sophistication is remarkable." In a sense, Aretha, through the sheer impressiveness of her instrument, a kind of vocal appeal agreeable to anyone with ears, helped to raise the musical sophistication of white audiences at the same time as she reminded black listeners, who weren't necessarily regular churchgoers, that they had a musical heritage of which they could be proud.

I'd argue that gospel is as much the quintessential American art form as the blues, and perhaps is even more so than jazz, since it lacks jazz's somewhat highbrow aesthetic and occasionally Eurocentric sensibility. That said, it is somewhat surprising that the authority of gospel is never questioned, that its foibles are so seldom exposed, that people are on eggshells around gospel. Religious music, it seems, cannot be criticized. If you're white and you question the sanctity of gospel, you're a borderline racist; if you're black and do so, you're a heathen.

That was the conundrum Aretha Franklin had grappled with in 1960 when she decided to follow in the footsteps of two of her idols, Cooke and Dinah Washington, and "go pop." Aretha's brother Cecil recalled that, "There was some conflict in the church congregation concerning her crossing over. They felt that to some degree she was turning her back on the church or on God, by singing secular music. My father played quite an instrumental role in raising people's enlightenment."

Indeed, C. L. Franklin did not see gospel and secular music as necessarily mutually exclusive. Asked once about the gospel/blues dichotomy, he said, "I always liked blues. There were some people, some church people who didn't approve it, blues, but they didn't understand that it was part of their cultural history." And for Aretha personally, the idea that the blues was a vital musical form that could coexist with gospel wasn't an abstract concept; it was proven regularly in her living room.

In the 1950s—widely viewed as the golden age of gospel— this vocal art was taken to new heights by women like Mahalia Jackson and Clara Ward, both of whom were fixtures in the C. L. Franklin household. Clara even dated C. L. in the mid- to late fifties. Mahalia famously changed Aretha's diapers.

Jackson was perhaps the most recognizable gospel singer of the twentieth century, a self-made success born into poverty in New Orleans in 1911. She left her hometown as a teenager, heading for Chicago, where she gradually built a reputation singing in a number of local churches. She attracted the notice of Decca Records and began cutting tracks that, though deeply spiritual, were nonetheless characterized by a bluesy feel Mahalia had appropriated from Bessie Smith, whom she revered, and transformed into her own signature style.

Though she never "left the church," as going pop is routinely, somewhat severely referred to, and though her commitment to sacred singing was never called into question, Mahalia was a physical singer, a sexual singer, whose performances dripped with sensuality (though tall, large, thick-bodied Mahalia hardly fit anyone's typical notions of sexy). In that respect, she fit right in to the Franklin family's world in which sanctity, celebrity, and down-home good times naturally coexisted. She too, like Reverend Franklin, was an intimate of Martin Luther King Jr., whom she helped convince to come to her hometown for the so-called Chicago Campaign of 1966. Mahalia and C. L. found themselves at the center of a fascinating axis of civil rights, spirituality, and sensuality, and the idea that racial pride, deep religious faith, and a life in music (with all the potential for irreligious activity it brought with it) were key ingredients to fulfillment was one that would profoundly inform Aretha's professional and personal identity.

If Mahalia was a close family friend and genuine influence on young Aretha, the singer's true idol, the woman she revered above all other vocalists, was Philadelphia native Clara Ward. Like Aretha, Clara was ushered into a singing career by a devout yet stage-parentish progenitor. In Clara's case, the Svengali was her irrepressible mother, Gertrude, who turned her back for good on her impoverished work as a day laborer after a supposed visitation from the Lord in 1931, during which she was allegedly instructed to spread His word. She instantly enlisted her two young daughters, Clara and Willa, to sing the gospel with her; Clara, the more talented, quickly became the family star. The Wards enlisted other singers, most notably the redoubtable Marion Williams, and famously hooked up with gospel-music composer W. Herbert Brewster, recording his "Surely, God Is Able," which would prove to be his signature song as well as that of the Wards. Brewster did much of the group's early songwriting, but Clara herself was a talented arranger and she also started composing songs. As a composer-arranger-interpreter, Clara would prefigure and influence her young friend and gospel associate, Aretha Franklin, who eventually, with her Atlantic Records association, would serve as singer, pianist, composer, arranger, and—that elusive yet, in the music business, all-important title—producer.

Aretha's teenage gospel record and performances were

strongly reminiscent of Ward's renditions of gospel standards. Imitation aside, the fourteen-year-old heard on these recordings is scarily precocious. The voice is at once youthful-sounding and somehow world-wise. And when teen Ree gets the spirit and delivers a daring, inspired, and impassioned octaves-spanning riff, it's every bit as astonishing as the vocal acrobatics she would unleash as an adult. Even a casual listener of Ward's records would be able to detect how vividly she influenced Aretha's singing; "There Is a Fountain Filled with Blood" in particular is almost identical to Ward's version.

Heilbut has aptly and hilariously described Clara's voice as "freakishly resonant," and it's true that the almost Indian-looking singer had a natural technique that, if it didn't always produce the most beautiful tone, gave her voice a point of focus that both carried well and recorded effectively. Aretha's tone, then and now, is breathier, less intense and focused, and her mezzo-soprano voice is placed a little higher than Clara's alto. But their similar ways with a riff, of taking time with a lyric, of punctuating a musical idea with an unpredictable but incisive wail or moan are uncanny. Like Aretha, Clara was a natural pianist, though she was decidedly less prodigious on the instrument than her protégé (as a child she stuck mainly to the black keys, while preteen Aretha could play virtually anything by ear). It's an oft-told story that Aretha decided to become a singer after witnessing a fervent Clara Ward, tearing through "Peace in the Valley" at a funeral, pull her hat off her head and throw it fiercely onto the ground beside the coffin, impressing the young girl with her passion (and perhaps inspiring adult Aretha's recent ponytail-launching routine). (There's a similar tale in which Clara, singing at Mahalia's 1972 funeral—Aretha sang too—hurled her fur stole directly at the coffin, which, in gospel circles, was viewed as a not inappropriate demonstration of love and respect.)

In a biography of her sister, Willa Ward-Royster declares that Clara was not just an inspiration to Aretha, she was a fan of C. L.'s daughter as well, having experienced young Aretha's gift first-hand as a performing member of Reverend Franklin's gospel tours. She writes that Clara could clearly see that "Aretha had an inherent gift from Mother Africa or Mother Earth, a gift that increased in value every passing day," tellingly attributing to Aretha's voice a kind of uncanny, elemental force, tracing it as the genealogical offspring of a celestial—and female—being. Describing the teenage Aretha, Ward-Royster continues, "No one could have taught her how to reach back up to where heart joins soul, gather the treasures trembling there, and then, song by song, present her glory to the listening world. Here was this shy, unaffected child who could without plan yank the covers off folks' emotions."

In her own autobiography, Aretha returns the compliment, professing her stalwart adulation of Clara, though she spends less time on how she was influenced musically than on certain ladylike tips her idol passed along: "I observed how [Clara] picked up a chicken leg and, instead of devouring it—like I would have—handled it very delicately. Extending her pinkie, she took small, ladylike bites. In contrast, I had more of a common grip."

This may seem hilariously off-message, but it nevertheless made sense that Aretha would rely on Clara for advice womanly as well as vocal. Clara's affair with C. L. was an open secret (Ward-Royster calls it "my sister's one and only heart, soul, and flesh real romance," though she also mentions that Clara, like a surprising number of gospel singers, occasionally "dabbled in homosexual activities"), and Clara became something of a surrogate mother to young Ree. Indeed, after Clara died in 1973, a notebook was discovered in which she had jotted down her impressions of everyone from other performers with whom she crossed paths to close personal friends. "My baby Aretha," she wrote. "She doesn't know how good she is. Doubts self. Some day—to the moon. I love that girl."

Aretha loved Clara as a maternal figure, as a singer, and also as one of gospel's purveyors of a true showbiz ethos. Much to the consternation of gospel purists, Clara Ward and the Ward Singers (who included mother

73

Gertrude, sister Willa, and, of course, gospel goddess Marion Williams, who also spent much time at the Franklin homestead) didn't perform only in traditional gospel robes; they wore sequined gowns of the variety more often seen on the Vegas strip than on the center aisle of a church. Hair (or wig) was piled high, skyward. When Clara first started making significant money in the late forties, her first major purchase was a green, fishtail Cadillac. In the midfifties, wealthier still, she upgraded to a twelve-passenger purple Chrysler.

Reverend James Cleveland's impact on Aretha was decidedly less showy but just as instructive. From James Aretha picked up little in the way of vocal technique—though an effective singer, the Reverend's sound was gruff and raspy and not particularly flexible. But if he had some vocal shortcomings, as a musical mind and pianist James was virtually without peer in the gospel world. (Listen to Aretha's *Amazing Grace* album, recorded live at Cleveland's New Temple Missionary Baptist Church in Los Angeles in 1972, to hear his soulful singing on "Precious Memories" and his fierce pianism throughout.) What takes Aretha beyond the mere realm of great singer and into the rarefied terrain of bona fide musical genius is her superlative skill at the piano, and most of the credit in this area is due to Reverend Cleveland. "He showed me some real nice chords, and I liked his deep, deep sound," Aretha has said. Reverend James taught young Ree the "striding, foot-stomping kind of piano," full of big, complex chords and a kind of provocative tension, which she would later employ in her greatest work.

Thus influenced by sensual and stentorian Mahalia, razzle-dazzle Clara, and virtuosic Reverend Cleveland, it makes perfect sense that Aretha found the borders separating gospel, blues, jazz, and pop to be malleable to say the least. And the fact that she excelled vocally at each genre made the decision to endeavor toward mainstream success that much more of a no-brainer. Plus, she'd already seen two close friends make the leap.

Dinah Washington was not as much of a fixture in the Franklin household as other famous musicians, but she was an occasional visitor, and she was certainly one of Aretha's favorite singers. The fact that she started her musical career as Ruth Jones, gospel pianist and singer, only added fuel to Aretha's already burning crossover fire. As a young woman, Dinah (still Ruth at the time) accompanied the thin-voiced gospel first lady Sallie Martin (around whom Ruth could sing circles) on the piano and eventually became a solo vocalist in her own right, before hooking up with Lionel Hampton and embarking on a jazz career. Dinah, a dynamic stage presence and singer, came to be known as the Queen of the Blues, though her biggest hits, pop fare like "What a Diff'rence a Day Makes," were characterized by lush strings and treacly arrangements that may have helped Dinah cross over but did little to enhance her earthy, forceful, gospel-trained sound. Listening to Washington, it's easy to hear the church strength in her voice, but its effect is subtle; Dinah didn't necessarily bring her gospel roots to the fore explicitly, the way Ray Charles did and Aretha would after him.

Washington is still one of Aretha's favorite singers: Ahmet Ertegun says that every time he visits Franklin at her Detroit home, they while away the hours eating Aretha's home cooking and listening to Dinah's records. And Ted White, a longtime friend of Washington's who used to bring her to the Franklin house, says that Dinah, in return, duly noted young Aretha's talent. "Women are very catty," White says. "They'll see a girl who's dressed very well and they'll say, Yeah, but look at those shoes, or look at that hairdo. Aretha was the only singer I've ever known that Dinah had no negative comments about. She just stood with her mouth open when she heard Aretha sing."

Aretha worshiped Dinah and went to see her perform at Detroit's Flame Show bar whenever she was in town (and underage Aretha could sneak in). Though she modeled her vocals after Clara's, the similarities between Aretha's and Dinah's jazzy-gospel styles are unmistakable: the laid-back timing, the slight earthy rasp in the vocal production, the sudden improvisational flights and wails. But the common musical ground between the two singers seems more the product of a shared background and career trajectory, plus a similar raspy-sweet timbre, than evidence of Aretha fashioning herself as a Dinah Washington imitator. If there was a pop singer Aretha did strive to emulate the way she did Clara's gospel delivery, it was Sam Cooke.

Sam was another intimate of the Franklin family, a sometime singer in C. L.'s church and, occasionally, on his gospel tours. If Aretha is perhaps the greatest female practitioner of gospel-soul vocalism, Cooke was her male counterpart. A twenty-year-old Sam started his professional show business career as the lead-singing replacement for the legendary R. H. Harris of the Soul Stirrers. His were unenviable shoes to fill considering Harris was one of the most influential (though least known) singers of the twentieth century. But Sam was up to the task vocally, as well as from a charisma standpoint: His good looks and natural sex appeal had female congregants (and some male ones too) thinking decidedly irreligious thoughts.

Aretha, too, like everyone else, was not exactly immune to this seductive combination of charm and talent, and she and her sisters, as teens, became rabid, squealing Sam Cooke groupies. But Aretha had an advantage over other Cooke fans, namely the fact that he was routinely present at her dinner table. Franklin had a serious crush on Sam Cooke, and though he was eleven years older than she was, there have been rumors, denied by Lady Soul, that the pair had some sort of romance at one point or another.

Whether the two singers became intimate or not, Aretha certainly absorbed Cooke's gritty, sexy, sweet singing style, to the point where she occasionally sounded even more like a Cooke clone than a Ward wannabe. "I was so influenced by him that Daddy told me to stop emulating Sam and instead express my own heart and soul," she says. Aretha eventually shed Cooke's vocal signatures in favor of her own, but the importance Sam placed on truly feeling, believing in whatever material he essayed was a lesson that would stay with her.

In 1956 Cooke left the Soul Stirrers and eased into the pop field with "Touch the Hem of His Garment," a lightly rocking, self-penned pop-gospel number that, although it was his solo record debut, was hardly a radical departure from his earlier church-music repertoire. Cooke quickly moved even deeper into the secular arena, scoring his first number-one pop hit, "You Send Me," in 1957, a move that triggered pop-chart envy in Aretha. Franklin told writer Gerri Hirshey of her affection for Sam: "Ooh, I loved that man. And when I saw he went pop, you know, outside the church, that's what made me say, 'I want to sing that stuff, too.'"

She wasn't alone. But as gospel chords, rhythms and feelings began to emerge on mainstream radio in the mid-1950s, it was clear that there were two true kings of this new brand of church-pop: Cooke and Ray Charles. Indeed, Charles is the name most often invoked along with Aretha's in discussions of the gospel-pop marriage. "She picked it up where Ray Charles started it and she conveyed it to a broader segment of the audience," Jerry Wexler told me, referring to the churchy inroads the two singers made in the pop field.

Like Aretha, Charles was a piano prodigy, a singing machine, and a performer who seemingly oozed emotion. When Ray released "I Got a Woman," with its driving gospel structure matched to salacious (for the era) lyrics, in 1955, it was nothing short of revolutionary. No soul singer has failed to be influenced by Ray in some way, but it's important to acknowledge, I think, that Aretha Franklin, despite the constant comparisons to Ray and the genuine debt she owes him as a trailblazer, is much more a Sam Cooke disciple than a Ray Charles follower. In the two schools of straight-from-the-church soul that emerged during this period, Aretha occupies a kind of middle ground between Cooke's urban, northern feel and Charles's grittier, southern vibe. Looking at Aretha's emergence from the gospel fold toward a mainstream stardom, it's important to align her with the proper influences. The singer has tremendous respect, love, and admiration for Ray Charles, but she wanted to *be* Sam Cooke (if she couldn't have him for herself, that is). Franklin sings like Cooke, with the same heartbreaking, tear-inducing combination of power, pathos, sweetness, and sex. The gospel influences so clear in Aretha's early Atlantic releases are more a matter of feel, sensibility, and improvisational instinct than they are literal extrapolations of actual gospel numbers (as Brother Ray's ingenious transformation of "This Little Light of Mine" into "This Little Girl of Mine" was, for example). Aretha and Ray will no doubt forever be linked—and rightfully so—as the mother and father of gospel-rooted R&B, but their individual musical sensibilities merely overlapped; they were not the same.

Despite some outrage at his so-called "blasphemous" move into secular music, Ray Charles, for the most part, would remain perpetually beloved in all sectors of the black community, perhaps because his Southern earthiness gave him an air of unassailable authenticity. Sam Cooke's pop-music ambitions, on the other hand, would forever rupture his ties to the church. Once he crossed over, he could never go back. Aretha, though she didn't know it at the time, would be one of the lucky ones. "Aretha Franklin is unusual," says Dr. Horace Boyer, a gospel historian and the author of *How Sweet the Sound*.

"Aretha has made two successful gospel recordings since she's been a soul singer. And gospel-music people love her just as much. They've kind of forgiven her." Cooke may have been shunned and Sister Rosetta Tharpe may have had a sparsely attended funeral (shocking for a onetime gospel artist of her stature; gospel stars habitually enjoy—if that's the right word—grand, monumental last rites). Aretha, however, would have pop success and somehow manage the feat of keeping the church world in her corner. There were certainly disgruntled sacred musicians who disapproved of her decision to become what one church diva scornfully called "a nightclub singer," but these naysayers were relatively few and far between. Perhaps it was her father's influence. Perhaps it was because of the emotional immediacy of her singing. Perhaps it was because, with her first big hits for Atlantic Records, Aretha *was* in effect singing the gospel. At Columbia, her gospel influence was apparent but muted; at Atlantic, on the other hand, Aretha had church every time she opened her mouth. How could gospel people begrudge her success when she was seemingly praising the Lord even when she might, literally, be berating a wayward lover? She couldn't have known she'd be able to sustain the admiration of her gospel peers when she signed with Columbia Records. What she did know was that her voice was God-given and church-nurtured, and no matter what she sang—whether she continued in the jazz-pop vein Columbia had established for her or headed in new directions—she would be sure to infuse her material with spirit. She didn't know any other way.

five

The New Deal

I remember she sang 'Respect,'" recalls Louise Bishop, the daughter of a sharecropper who rose to the House of Representatives and thus knows a thing or two about the esteem Aretha demanded in what would become her signature song. "And I just could not believe that anybody could sing that song better than Otis Redding."

Representative Bishop isn't alone in deeming Franklin's interpretation of Redding's song superior to Otis's own funky, deeply soulful original version. What's striking about the comment is that Bishop is referring to a live performance of "Respect" almost a full year before Aretha's Atlantic Records cover of the song helped anoint her Lady Soul. Aretha had added "Respect" to her set list before she even left Columbia, at a time when she had recently recorded such radically different material as

"Swanee" and "Ol' Man River" for the label. But it was "Respect" that sparked an idea in Bishop's mind.

As a well-known radio personality at Philadelphia's WDAS Radio and a future minister involved in the black church, Bishop had almost inevitably crossed paths with Aretha and her family and was a fan, not just of Franklin's Columbia records but, particularly, of her gospel work. When Aretha booked gigs at Philly's Cadillac Club in early 1966, Bishop made sure to check her out.

"It was a very tiny club, probably seated two hundred fifty people," Bishop remembers. "But her singing was so close to church singing that I was just in love with her." So much so that Bishop caught nearly every show of an almost week-long engagement. "The last night she was there I said, 'Aretha, what are you going to do with yourself? You don't have a contract anymore!' She said, 'I'm going to record myself. I'm just as good a singer as Barbra Streisand, and I've not had the push behind me that she has. I can sing anything she can sing—and better.'

"So I said, 'Aretha, you're much too big a singer to record yourself. You're an artist! I know somebody. Why don't you let me introduce you?'"

It was Jerry Wexler that Bishop had in mind, another inevitable acquaintance for a disk jockey, especially considering born schmooze Wexler had enjoyed careers all over the music-world map as writer, promoter, and producer.

"I used to call Jerry Mr. Atlantic," Bishop told me. "I absolutely thought he was the greatest soul producer there was. I knew that Jerry's talent was exactly what Aretha needed, so making the marriage, performing the ceremony between Jerry and Aretha, was a natural."

Aretha certainly had no objections to being hooked up with Wexler, who at the time was perhaps the biggest producer in the world. Her husband, Ted White, had engaged in casual negotiations with Mercury Records, so Franklin had a sense that there would be a label home for her if she wanted. But as White says, Mercury "was kind of our ace in the hole. We were going to shop around. And Atlantic was one of the companies we were interested in." Bishop quickly went to work bringing her two friends together. "When I got home that night, it was one o'clock in the morning," she continues. "But it was not unusual for me to call his house at one or for him to call mine if there was something good happening that we wanted to share. So I called Jerry's house, and Shirley, his wife then, answered the phone and said Jerry was in Muscle Shoals, recording. I said, 'I just left Aretha Franklin, and she's interested in talking to Jerry. Have him call me.' Within five minutes Jerry was on the phone. Shirley had gotten out of her bed evidently and called Jerry to tell him Aretha was without contract and she wanted to talk to him."

Jerry, it's true, was thrilled to get the news about Aretha.

He'd had his eye on her for some time. Her effervescent and virtuosic teen recording of the gospel classic "Precious Lord" had knocked him out, and while he was for the most part confounded by the A&R decisions Columbia continued to impose on her, he nevertheless admired her recording of "Today I Sing the Blues" and loved "If Ever I Would Leave You," from *Camelot*. "I knew all her records, and I knew all about her. I was just waiting for her contract to run out," Wexler recalls today. "There was no aggressively pursuing her—she's under contract! But I was friends with Louise, and I said to her, Listen, I'm not begging you for a greasy favor, but if you know when she's free, let me know."

Like so many others, Bishop relishes the opportunity to imitate Wex's singular, nasal, penetrating, Washington Heights hepcat accent. "So he called me," recalled Bishop, affecting Jerry's twang, "and he said, 'What's huh numbah?!'" I gave him her number and the rest is history."

Jerry remembers that he contacted Aretha immediately on the heels of Bishop's referral. But, in fact, he'd already had business dealings with Franklin's camp. The first artist Wexler brought down to Muscle Shoals to record at Fame Studios was Wilson Pickett, and one of the first hits Pickett cut there was "Mustang Sally." To get the rights to the tune, Wexler had been in touch with Ted White, whose publishing company, Fourteenth Hour, owned the song.

"That song was written by a neighbor of mine at the time called Sir Mack Rice," White told me. "He sang with the Falcons, but he had stopped his show business career and was driving a truck. He would bring songs around to us, and we would write together—good writer, writes real funky. He brought 'Mustang Mama' to me, and we changed the title and a couple of lines here and there, and it became 'Mustang Sally.'"

In fact, in 2002 Rice told the *Detroit Free Press* that it was Aretha herself who suggested the fortuitous name change from "Mama" to "Sally." It's easy to believe, considering the song's "ride, Sally, ride" refrain comes from the same African-American children's rhyme, "Little Sally Walker," that would also provide the inspiration for a verse of Aretha's composition "Spirit in the Dark," released four years later. As a mother to young children, Aretha clearly had nursery rhymes on the brain; her personal, day-to-day life informed her creative decisions.

Between Louise Bishop and "Mustang Sally," Jerry and Aretha were seemingly destined to talk business at some point. Wexler wasted no time in calling Aretha from Muscle Shoals and set up a meeting in his New York office as soon as he got back to town. By all accounts the negotiations, such as they were, following Aretha's fall 1966 release from Columbia, couldn't have gone more smoothly. "She and Ted White sat down in my office," Wexler said.

"No lawyers, managers, or agents in sight—and we made a handshake deal. It was beautiful." It was the first time Wex had met Ree in the flesh and the producer was struck by the singer's presence. "She was gorgeous," Wexler told me. "She was very pretty, personable, and intelligent. She's very smart. She didn't run over with excitement. It was business: Okay, let's make some records."

White too remembers that aligning Aretha and Atlantic was straightforward. About Jerry he says, "I was impressed. He was a very open-minded person, very easy to talk to. And he had his finger on the pulse. It was a pleasure to work with Jerry."

It was a good thing that White appreciated and respected Wexler, because the Atlantic executive's first, somewhat provocative idea for Aretha was to bring her down South. In fact, "send" her down South would be more accurate, for originally Jerry had no intention of producing the session. Wex is so indelibly linked in the soul-music cultural consciousness, in such a hands-on way, to Aretha's Atlantic emergence, that it's hard to believe he initially had no plan to produce Franklin himself. Between Pickett and other Muscle Shoals and New York sessions he was superintending, not to mention his preoccupation with the idea of selling the company, he was simply too busy to accompany his new label signee into the studio.

"My first instinct was to offer her to Jim Stewart and have the Stax team produce her," Wexler wrote. "No one figured to produce Aretha any better than those good folks in Memphis." Wexler told label president Stewart that he could record the young singer as an exclusive Stax artist; Atlantic would provide marketing and distribution services to insure that whatever funky tracks were recorded at Stax's Memphis studio (and the label was on a serious funk roll) would get widely heard. Considering Wexler was tormented over his earlier decision to sign Redding over to Stax, it is surprising that he was prepared to do the same with the woman who would become Otis's spiritual sister of sorts. It's fascinating to contemplate what Aretha's output would have been had she gone to Stax. The label had had recent (and enduring) successes with such artists as Sam and Dave ("Hold On, I'm Comin'"), Carla Thomas ("Gee Whiz"), and of course Redding, whose chart-burning Stax tenure was inaugurated with "These Arms of Mine," and included such classics as "Mr. Pitiful," "Try a Little Tenderness," and later (posthumously) "(Sittin' on) The Dock of the Bay." Memphis, where Stax was housed in a converted movie theater, was Aretha's birthplace, and the Southern funk at which the studio excelled was perfectly suited to her gospel-born gifts. Motown would never have worked for Aretha, but Stax, where the house band was Booker T. and the

MGs, where Redding cut the original "Respect" (and indeed all his major hits), and where keyboard whiz Isaac Hayes was developing a production style and musical sensibility that would make him one of the most important soul artists of the early 1970s—Stax could have done some damage with Aretha Franklin.

But, alas, it was not to be. As Wexler put it, "Stewart passed. Thank you, Jesus."

Wexler goes gospel in that comment because Aretha's first dozen Atlantic releases would prove to be among the producer's most enduring legacies. Though it's hard to conceive, years after their momentously fruitful association, that Jerry Wexler would have been reluctant to produce Aretha himself, once enlisted, he took to the task wholeheartedly. In fact, he found himself operating in a more direct, active way than he had with any other artist before: "In Aretha's case, fate, fortune, or the pull of my own passion led me into the studio with her to work in a more involving way than I had ever worked before." Wexler enjoyed a reputation as a song-selection genius, and his marathon sessions poring over possible tunes for each of his artists are legendary. But for the Aretha project, he would find himself a significant participant in the collaborative interplay among the musicians on the studio floor, a musical coming-together hardly unheard of but notably electrifying as it occurred on Aretha's early Atlantic sessions.

The first decision Jerry made about Aretha's Atlantic debut was that the recording should happen in the South— if not in Memphis, at Stax, then in Muscle Shoals, where he'd recently had such success with Pickett. Ted White wasn't initially delighted at the idea: "With the racial situation at that time, I was a bit reluctant," he says thirty-seven years later. "I'd never heard of [Muscle Shoals], really. I just had heard the results of some of the things that had been done down there." White's trepidation was hardly unjustified. Muscle Shoals is about 120 miles from Birmingham, site of the incendiary 1963 segregation protests that led to a church bombing that killed four young girls; a little more than 200 miles from Montgomery, site of the 1955 to 1956 Rosa Parks–inspired bus boycott; and about 225 miles from Selma, where thousands protested the beating and killing of a black minister by white segregationists in 1965. There was scarcely another state in the union with a more problematic recent racial history. Northwest Alabama, where Muscle Shoals is located, had been a Ku Klux Klan stronghold, and though the Klan's influence had waned dramatically, and though Florence, Alabama's school integration had gone without a hitch, with scarcely so much as a phone call placed to police, the region was nevertheless not the first place you would think of to take a young black woman you were trying to make comfortable and to welcome into a new working environment.

Wexler was not insensitive to racial issues like these, but his was a color-blind MO that took him where the funk was, and in the mid-1960s, Memphis and Muscle Shoals were where the most soulful players were to be found. Jerry's feeling that Fame would provide the right environment for Ree wasn't based on mere convenience, cost concerns, or the fact that he'd started to become friendly with the Muscle Shoals musicians. Wex was enamored of both Aretha's gospel work and her Columbia recordings, and he knew that the former was where her astonishing talent truly shone.

Working with jaded New York session players would produce too slick a sound. That had been part of the problem with Aretha's Columbia product, Wexler thought. Her occasionally high-type tendencies (a kind of striving toward sophisticated, Nancy Wilsonesque pop and away from bluesier influences) were indulged when recording pop and jazz material up North. To do justice to Aretha's talents required that he bring the gospel in Aretha, as well as her down-home ragged edges, to the fore. He knew Aretha played piano (though at this point he didn't know quite how well), a talent Columbia had neglected to exploit. He suspected that putting Aretha at the piano, in a Southern studio where the players knew gospel and the blues, that giving her emotional vocal presentation free rein, might be the key to cutting hot tracks. Jerry says he was more directly involved in the Aretha sessions than any other he had produced, but perhaps his most astute production decision was to step back and let Aretha's talent lead the way. He was intimately involved in song selection, in determining what circumstances Aretha needed to produce her best work, and in orchestrating the sessions, but Jerry's participation was a kind of shadow, behind-the-scenes involvement, if you could call it that. "He knew that she couldn't be contained," says David Ritz, who coauthored both Wexler's and Aretha's autobiographies and thus has a unique take on their work together. "He knew to just roll with the vocals, let her musical vision prevail."

The best way to do that, Wexler believed, was to provide the singer with musical support at once funky, capable, eager, and laid-back. These were the qualities he had discovered in Alabama, where Jerry had almost instantly become besotted with the Muscle Shoals scene. The results on the Pickett sessions spoke for themselves, and though Fame honcho Rick Hall could be tough to take, Wex quickly found himself enjoying a kind of paternalistic affection for the Alabama musicians, most of whom were in their early twenties, while he was pushing fifty. It didn't hurt, either, that they revered him, were in fact terrified of this Jewish New York dynamo who had, in essence, descended on their backwater turf and enabled them to be heard by millions the world over. Ritz is an avowed Wexler devotee who speaks of the man with tremendous affection. As he jokingly points out, "Jerry was like a pig in shit down there. They were all kissing his ass like crazy—which he loves! Jerry loves him some adulation, and he was getting adulated up the ying-yang."

It's true. Even today, the musicians on those early Muscle Shoals sessions speak about Jerry Wexler in reverential tones. Jimmy Johnson, who played guitar on Aretha's *I Never Loved a Man* sessions, as well as her next few albums for Atlantic, can't give Jerry enough credit for his work in Muscle Shoals, contradicting Rick Hall's assertion that no one considered him a music producer as much as an executive. Johnson, an easy-going, good-natured Alabaman, recalls being alternately admiring and terrified of Wexler. "I was scared to fuckin' death. I mean we could hardly talk to him," Jimmy told me of his first few Pickett sessions with Wexler. "I was scared to death he was going to ask me to play something I wasn't gonna know how to play. And sure enough, he comes over to me, and I'm just about to pass out." Here Johnson begins trading in his Southern drawl for Wexler's New Yawkese. " 'Jimmy, can you give me a little *giggy-giggy-gongy-gongy*? And I'm thinking, my God, what the hell is *giggy-giggy-gongy-gongy*? I mean, I didn't get it. It was a rhythm pattern. Five years later I would have known. I thought it was some kind of Chinese-Jewish thing. *Giggy-giggy-gongy-gongy*. What the hell? I could see my career ending because I couldn't *giggy-giggy-gongy-gongy*. So I did the fastest thinking a slow redneck ever did in his life, and I said, 'What about this, Jerry?' And I went into some other lick, and he said, 'Jimmy, I like that.' I could have kissed him."

All the Muscle Shoals guys have similarly harrowing and hilarious Wexler tales, and it's a tribute to the relationships born in this period that Wexler maintains close friendships with almost all the musicians who played on *I Never Loved a Man*. Guitarist and songwriter Chips Moman now lives in Georgia, but he and Jerry speak once a month, virtually without fail. Jimmy Johnson got married a few years ago; shortly after his wedding he brought his new bride to East Hampton to meet the famous Jerry Wexler. Keyboard player Spooner Oldham, when I first called and told him Wexler had referred me, instantly inquired, "Oh, Jerry! How's he doing?" before I'd so much as given my name. In December 1966, as Wexler prepared to bring Aretha down for her first sessions, he couldn't have known that these twentysomething Southern boys he'd chosen to work with the future Queen of Soul would become lifelong friends. But he must have sensed somehow that these were musicians he could trust, who were capable of good work, who could help create a vibe in which Aretha would feel free to express herself in ways she never had at Columbia.

And Lord knows, Aretha was eager to express herself. The idea that she had been profoundly, unfairly stifled at Columbia, that she had been a virtual prisoner of the label's whimsical and ineffective A&R schemes has been largely overblown. Aretha herself has said as much. But the fact is that "Dr. Feelgood" and the other original songs on *I Never Loved a Man the Way I Love You* didn't just appear out of thin air the moment Franklin set foot in the studio with Wexler. Aretha was steering herself in a new direction by adding songs like "Respect" to her supperclub set. And before the Columbia contract expired, she had been working on new material and saving it for the proverbial rainy day. Her Columbia producer Clyde Otis wasn't even aware of the songs she was writing. "She didn't tell me [about the songs]," Otis says. "She put those songs in her trunk or wherever."

Ted White confirms that there were regular songwriting sessions during the period leading up to Aretha's liberation from Columbia. "We had this gigantic source of material we had put together," he recalls rather grandiosely (Aretha's original output on Atlantic over the course of a dozen years was not insignificant, but it was hardly as if she recorded only her own material). "We'd go up into the attic, an old rec room, and we'd take our writers up there—we'd have maybe eight or ten people over. And we'd start a song, and whoever could contribute would contribute. It was like a party thing. We'd do this maybe three times a week. And sometimes, she and I alone would sit down at the piano. And she'd be working on her thing, and I'd help her with the lyrics." The result of these regular efforts, if not a vast catalog of potential hits, as White to some degree suggests, was a handful of tunes that were certainly worth recording and that revealed a side of Aretha's talent that had lain dormant.

Aretha had new material she felt excited about and a yearning for hits—more important, she had the chops to support her ambition and a growing need to express herself in a new way. Wexler had the necessary star-making machinery in place, and he'd discovered a studio, a quasi-Arcadian musical world unto itself (or so it seemed at the time), where tracks could be produced that merited the hype. Jerry and Aretha's union, as brought about by Louise Williams Bishop, had been painless to say the least. An offer had been extended and accepted. Songs had been chosen (selection, according to White, "was kind of a collaboration, a big family affair. It was a party."). All that remained was to get down to work. "Why don't you let me introduce you?" Louise Bishop had implored Aretha, referring to Wexler and Atlantic. "They would understand you. They would hear you, and know where you need to be, and put you in the right vein." She was right.

six

Muscle Shoals, Alabama

*M*uscle Shoals is not in most guidebooks. The Tennessee River rapids for which the town is named are no longer a hazard, having been tamed by an elaborate network of dams built in the 1920s and 1930s. Visitors to this northwest region of the Camellia State are more likely to investigate nearby Florence, which is just across the Tennessee and is the site of Frank Lloyd Wright's Rosenbaum House, recently reopened to the public, and home to the annual W. C. Handy Music Festival. Or visit Tuscumbia, Helen Keller's birthplace, where *Miracle Worker* fans make pilgrimages for the yearly Keller festival to see William Gibson's play staged under the stars at Keller's childhood home, the idyllically named Ivy Green. Sheffield, the fourth of the loose consortium of towns known as the Shoals, has perhaps the least in the way of a tourist draw.

The character of the Shoals is largely defined by the Tennessee, from which one can see the gently rolling Appalachian Mountains, covered in forest. The area has a rich Native American history, having been originally inhabited by the Chickasaw tribe. In 1921, the prehistoric appeal of the Shoals was under threat of compromise by the wish of Henry Ford to transform the area into a major city, where he intended to locate his car-empire headquarters. The plan was eventually scrapped, but not before the groundwork for the town had been laid; much of Muscle Shoals as it exists today is a result of Ford's conception. The Alcoa aluminum company has since established a presence in the town, but it's perhaps appropriate, or telling, that the major industrialization planned for the region in the early part of the last century was abandoned, for the charm of Muscle Shoals and its environs lies in its earthy, funky, and straight-up country origins. Local mythology holds that the area's knack for producing music of quality and spirit stems directly from its proximity to the Tennessee, which, according to Native American legend, sings.

Despite its virtually untouched, small-town charm, Muscle Shoals can't be said to generate a tremendous amount of excitement—unless you're a rhythm-and-blues musician trying to capture the unmistakable sound of Southern soul. That sound, and with it a local music industry, had started brewing here in the late fifties, with the release of James Joiner's "A Fallen Star," a country song that hit the top ten. That was all it took to lure Rick Hall and then partner Billy Sherrill to the region, as well as a number of other musicians and would-be producers. (Sherrill would later achieve renown as a producer and the co-writer of Tammy Wynette's "Stand by Your Man.") Nashville was still (and of course *is* still) the South's music mecca, but even in the fifties breaking into the Nashville scene was a challenge. Muscle Shoals and Florence provided an easier and more laid-back—but still musically vital—point of entry for an ambitious young performer or songwriter.

Ambitious was certainly the word for Rick Hall. A genuinely talented guitar player and all-around musician, Rick was, in those days, driven by his considerably healthy ego. "When you're young, you're eat up with ego," Hall concedes. "You think there's nothing you can't do." But it can't be said that his ambition didn't bear fruit, and by 1967, before he'd turned thirty-five, Hall was the chairman of the board of the Muscle Shoals scene. As the proprietor of Fame Studios—where Aretha would record—he had been developing a killer Southern backing band for some time, including impossibly mellow keyboardist Spooner Oldham; rhythm guitarist and sometime engineer Jimmy Johnson; trombone player-turned-bassist David Hood;

and the youthful-looking but powerful drummer Roger
Hawkins.

Oldham, Johnson, Hawkins, and Hood were all local
boys—they didn't need to migrate anywhere to insinuate
themselves into a happening music scene. By age twenty-
three, the laconic Spooner was a fixture at the square,
fortresslike brick building that was Fame Studios, where
he played regularly as a session keyboardist. He was also
under contract to Fame Publishing as a songwriter, and
was busy writing new material, often with his good buddy
Dan Penn. Together they composed "I'm Your Puppet,"
which would go on to be a hit for James and Bobby Purify
and be recorded by Marvin Gaye and other artists. The
song would elevate Spooner above the ranks of other aspiring writers in the region and make him a core member
of Hall's stable of musicians.

The same was true of Jimmy Johnson, officially the first
employee at the new Fame, where he initially worked as
Rick's "secretary." When he wasn't taking Hall's phone
messages, he was picking up his boss's castoff engineering
gigs and playing guitar on sessions, having abandoned
his original instrument, the trumpet, when, as a typically
hormonal teenager, he came to the enticing realization
that the guitar was shaped like the body of a woman.
Hall got the glory (and a considerable sum of money)
for bringing "When a Man Loves a Woman" to Jerry

Wexler's attention, but it was Johnson who recorded the track. "He allowed me to engineer sessions when he didn't want to do 'em," Jimmy says of Rick. He starts singing a tune: " 'Do you like good music, yeah man. Sweet soul music.' That was one of my early million sellers." These early successes, Alabama songs that would be heard the world over, remain endearingly fresh in the memories of the men behind them and a tremendous source of pride.

Roger Hawkins, also still a kid at the time of the Aretha session, was nonetheless a similarly capable musician. As a teenager he'd gone to Atlanta to gain experience, and when he came back, he was quickly hired by Fame and started playing drums on most sessions. An extremely talented and ultimately influential drummer, Hawkins, to some degree, didn't realize how good he was at the time. Hall wasn't forthcoming with compliments, and it wasn't until Jerry Wexler singled him out after cutting Pickett's "Land of 1,000 Dances," and anointed the young player "a great drummer," that Roger fully realized where his potential could take him in the music business. "There was a difference in Roger after that day—to the good," Jimmy Johnson recalls. "And I think other people started giving him more respect that day too." ("A good drummer always knows the lyrics of a song," Wexler told me. "Roger Hawkins *always* knew the lyrics to a song.")

Hawkins would ultimately become known as one half of one of the great rhythm sections in rock music, with bass player David Hood. But in 1967, not yet the influential bassist he would become, Hood found himself picking up gigs as a trombone player, and that was what he played on "I Never Loved a Man (the Way I Love You)." "I was just thrilled to death to get on any recording session," the Sheffield native recalls today. "I was just wantin' to be *in*. I was an aspiring player, and I was going to get on the scene any way—I didn't care if I was shakin' a tambourine." Hood would eventually go on to play bass for such artists as Paul Simon, Willie Nelson, Bob Seger, the Staples Singers, and other significant artists. But during the early Pickett-Franklin era in Muscle Shoals, he was determined to keep his mouth shut and wait for an opportunity. It's easy to imagine (though somewhat absurd in light of his later accomplishments) a bright, youthful David Hood, one of the more thoughtful, orderly and composed of the group (he still keeps his daily calendars with bookings from this era) sitting quietly on the couch in Fame's Studio A, content merely to be part of the action.

The musicians involved in the making of Aretha's Atlantic debut were not all from the Florence-Sheffield-Muscle Shoals axis, however. Spooner's sometime songwriting partner, Dan Penn, was a regular around Fame, but he was in fact an adjunct to a Memphis contingent of R&B

aficionados who were enlisted to play on Aretha's record. A terrific singer, Penn was considered the most soulful white man alive and a listener of unerring taste. ("In my mind, if Dan liked something, it was probably a hit," Hall says today. "Because he hated everything.") Penn hailed from Vernon, Alabama; as a teenager he was a regular on the northern Alabama music circuit, and after replacing Hall as lead singer of the Fairlanes, eventually went to work for his band's predecessor as a Fame songwriter. His first major song was a hit for Conway Twitty on the country charts, but Dan was into black music. "I was into R&B so heavy, I didn't listen to nothin' else," he told me. His songwriting credits, which include "Dark End of the Street" and "Do Right Woman"—both recorded by Aretha—are indicative of the common ground shared by classic country and classic R&B. Although much soul music is considered to be a cousin of jazz and blues, in many ways it is country, with its stripped-down, rural, everyman appeal, that is R&B's closest relative. As a singer and a composer, Penn perfectly embodied this musical overlap.

When Dan wasn't writing with Spooner, he occasionally paired with guitarist and producer Chips Moman, with whom he wrote "Do Right Woman—Do Right Man," which would be cut—in part, at least—by Aretha at her Muscle Shoals session. With his easygoing manner, ready laugh, and guitar chops, Chips was an in-demand player at studios in Memphis and Nashville, as well as Muscle Shoals. Jerry Wexler calls Chips "the most underappreciated guitarist in the South. Genius. He's got a great reputation as a get-it-together guy and an entrepreneur and a contractor and a dealmaker, and he's charismatic. He's the kind of guy you can't win an argument with—like Ted Williams. But nobody ever thinks of his guitar ability, because he doesn't put himself in the forefront."

When *I Never Loved a Man* happened, Chips had had his own Memphis studio, American Sound Studios, for several years; whereas the Muscle Shoals boys were still relatively green, Chips was something of an industry player. Moman's American Studios house band was behind literally dozens of recent hits, and Chips himself had also cut many of Stax's early records. It was during his tenure at that label that he met Wexler. "Jerry and I have been friends since the day we met," says Chips, who recalls that it was his work producing William Bell's "You Don't Miss Your Water" that first made Wexler a fan. "He's still a hero to me. I learned a lot about the business from Jerry."

If Jerry was helpful to Moman's career, the relationship was mutually beneficial. As a Stax fixture and player on countless records, Chips was connected to a significant stable of Memphis musicians, including his good friend Tommy Cogbill, who was enlisted to play bass on a litany of Muscle Shoals recordings (including Aretha's). (Of all the players on Aretha's first Atlantic record, Cogbill is the only one no longer living; he died of a brain aneurysm in 1983.) Consequently, it was Moman to whom Wexler turned with the task of putting together a horn section for the Aretha session. The first person Moman called was tenor sax player Charlie Chalmers, a Memphian at the center of a busy and thriving (if somewhat competitive) brass scene. "I was in the middle of a happening thing—several musicians and horn players that were working together. It was kind of a cliquey thing," says the disarmingly affable Charlie, who, a few years after working with Aretha, would solidify his still-developing reputation as a mainstay on the classic Al Green albums of the early seventies. It was on those recordings that Chalmers embarked on a second career of sorts, as a background singer; along with sisters Donna and Sandra Rhodes, Charlie made a name for the Rhodes Chalmers Rhodes backup group, which would provide the full, mixed-gender vocal sound so effective on Green's "Let's Stay Together" and other hits.

But in 1967, Chalmers was much more a sax player and horn arranger than a vocalist, and as a Memphian, he was a frequent collaborator of Chips and the obvious choice to get a horn crew together. For the Aretha Franklin session in Muscle Shoals, however, Charlie was unable to secure the involvement of his usual section, which generally included Floyd Newman on baritone sax and Bowlegs Miller on trumpet. "I was having a hard time getting the guys I normally played with," Chalmers says now in his sublimely resonant speaking voice. "We were having some kind of a competitive thing going on. There was a little attitude. So I was forced to get other players who read charts."

The horn section that did end up playing the gig was something of a hodgepodge: Chalmers on tenor sax, Hood on trombone, Joe Arnold, also on sax, and Ken Laxton on trumpet. Laxton was the wild card, a talented trumpeter who nevertheless was not well known to any of the other musicians. Moreover, this section was all white, whereas Chalmers's usual horn group was racially integrated. Rick Hall has historically taken the blame for ignoring Wexler's specific (and somewhat nervous) request for a mixed-race horn section on the Aretha Franklin sessions, but in fact, for that, he was not to blame.

It was odd to have a person on the floor with whom the rest of the guys were not on intimate musical terms. These Southern players, though they jumped from gig to gig and session to session, formed something of a makeshift family. It certainly made Jerry's preproduction work straightforward: A few calls to Rick Hall and Chips Moman, and he could be confident that when he arrived at the session he'd be greeted by a roomful of killer players who had spent considerable time nurturing a musical synergy among themselves. They hailed from Memphis, Florence, Sheffield, Muscle Shoals, Nashville, LaGrange—but musically they formed a kind of loose brotherhood that trafficked in a unique and, at the time, still developing brand of rhythm and blues. Under the tutelage of Jerry Wexler, their sound would reach millions. "Rick Hall gave us the chance and could be called the father of Muscle Shoals music," Jimmy Johnson says today. "But Wexler was the godfather, because he opened the international market for us."

It is indeed amazing to think that a group of mainly twentysomething Southern white boys, self-described rednecks, would in part provide the means for Aretha Franklin to become the Queen of Soul. But to industry insiders of this era working in this genre, the very definition of R&B was black artists working with white, Southern supporters. There even seems to exist a kind of semantic divide: Black listeners for the most part consider Aretha's music "soul"; white producers and musicians call it "rhythm and blues." Generally speaking, the terms have become interchangeable, but the semiotics of these rubrics points to the rather knotty racial subtext surrounding the making of much of this music. It's frankly a quasi-Utopian, harmonious (not to mention borderline hokey) vision of races coming together to produce art that would have a profound effect on a community. Working with Aretha Franklin and other black artists had a worldview-altering, racial-cultural impact on the Southern white boys who played on those records, and by extension, on the communities these young men hailed from; working with the musically gifted Southern white boys helped Aretha Franklin, surprisingly, have a profoundly empowering impact on the larger black culture as a whole.

Between them, Hall and Wexler had links to just about every rock-solid working musician in the South. But in January of 1967, Wexler wasn't yet the godfather of the local musical identity, as Jimmy Johnson calls him; he was still more of a talent developer and taker of cultural temperatures, a kind of R&B Bugsy Siegel surveying a swath of land in Nevada and determining to turn it into Las Vegas. Pickett had cut killer tracks with this outfit, and Wexler hoped to recreate that magic. If lightning struck twice, this time with Aretha, he had any number of artists he'd be delighted to give the Muscle Shoals treatment.

These players were young, but they had chops. Pickett, Percy, Arthur Alexander—these were not insignificant artists to cut one's teeth with. But if they were musically prepared to work with someone of Aretha's caliber, they nevertheless had no idea who she was. Fame's small lobby had a chalkboard calendar hanging on one wall, on which were written the names of artists with upcoming sessions. "I remember seeing her name on the schedule. I said, '*A*-retha who?'" Jimmy Johnson recalls, placing the emphasis on the name's first syllable. "I didn't even know how to say her name." Spooner remembers being similarly at a loss. "I knew minimal about her. And I definitely didn't know where she was going," he says. "But that was good. It meant we were coming from a fresh viewpoint."

If the Muscle Shoals guys had little knowledge of Aretha, the Memphians on the sessions were considerably more clued in. Chalmers knew a bit about the young singer ("I got the drift that Columbia wasn't recording her right, that it was kind of poppy, milquetoast."), and Dan Penn and Chips were full-fledged fans of the preacher's daughter. "I had heard her father on WLAC radio," Penn recalls, citing the Nashville R&B and gospel station. "I was a real heavy WLAC listener, so I kept up with all of the preachers and the singers. I had heard some of Aretha Franklin's Columbia records—smooth as glass, but not very exciting. It hid her fire. But I had heard her fire in the gospel stuff. I had heard her enough to know that, man, this girl was good."

111

Growing up in LaGrange, Georgia, Moman had been a gospel appreciator since the late 1940s; he too had some sense of what to expect from Aretha. "I'd been raving about Aretha since 1959. She was one of the greatest singers I ever heard, even back then. And I loved her when she was with the Ray Bryant Trio," Chips told me, referring to the jazz ensemble that played on Franklin's first few Columbia LPs, and launching into a verse from the rollicking, gospelesque "Won't Be Long," recorded when Aretha was eighteen. " 'Baby here I be's. By the railroad track.' It was a hell of a thing, and Tommy Cogbill and I would talk about what a real groove that was. That record could still hit. It could be a big record on her right now. Fact is, people would love to hear something fresh like that, cause that's fresh again. She floored me with that song first time I heard it." His reaction is understandable, and "Won't Be Long" is one of the songs from Franklin's Columbia tenure that give lie to the notion that everything she did for that label was slick pop-jazz devoid of Aretha's natural gospel feeling; "Won't Be Long" is pure gospel funneled into a blues-pop context.

For her part, Aretha would have little inkling of what to expect from the Muscle Shoals boys. She may have been born in Memphis, but she was a Northern girl, reared in Detroit and working in New York. Ted White trusted Wexler, but he was nevertheless wary of recording in

Teenage Aretha in Columbia Records' studios.

(Michael Ochs Archives.com)

Recording at Columbia. (FDR/Michael Ochs Archives.com)

TOP: Aretha.

(Harry Goodwin/Michael Ochs Archives.com)

BOTTOM: Aretha's father, the Reverend C. L. Franklin.

(Michael Ochs Archives.com)

TOP LEFT: Clara Ward, Aretha's number-one gospel influence.
(Michael Ochs Archives.com)

TOP RIGHT: Aretha's idol and crush Sam Cooke.
(Michael Ochs Archives.com)

BOTTOM: The Fame Studios building in the early 1970s. (Courtesy of Fame Studios)

The Muscle Boys in 1966. Back, from left: Tommy Cogbill, Chips Moman, Spooner Oldham, Roger Hawkins. Seated: bass player Junior Lowe, Wilson Pickett, Jimmy Johnson. (Courtesy of Jimmy Johnson Music)

The *I Never Loved a Man* session resumes at Atlantic's studio, February 1967.

(Photo: David Gahr)

Singing and playing at the *I Never Loved a Man* session.
(Photo: David Gahr)

A relaxed moment in the studio with husband Ted White.

(Photo: David Gahr)

With the then-ever-present cigarette.

(Photo: David Gahr)

Lady Soul. (Michael Ochs Archives.com)

TOP RIGHT: Fame's Rick Hall, with his growing gold-record collection. (Courtesy of Fame Studios)

BOTTOM RIGHT: Preparing to tape for one of many late-sixties television appearances. (Michael Ochs Archives.com)

Aretha records at Atlantic Studios, 1969.

TOP: Inside the Atlantic control room. From left: Ted White, Aretha, Wexler, Nesuhi Ertegun, Ahmet Ertegun. (Photo: David Gahr)

BOTTOM: Aretha at the piano. (Photo: David Gahr)

Wexler and Aretha with the singer's first gold records.

(Courtesy of Jerry Wexler)

TOP: Ree and Wex. (Courtesy of Jerry Wexler)

BOTTOM: Aretha and Jerry Wexler discuss an arrangement at Atlantic's studio.

(Courtesy of Jerry Wexler)

Aretha and Louise Williams Bishop look at a passage from the Bible.

(Courtesy of Louise Bishop)

a small Southern town. "I'd never heard of it, really," White says of Muscle Shoals. "I just had heard the results of some of the things that had been done down there—thought it might be a pretty good idea. But with the racial situation at that time, I was a bit reluctant, apprehensive."

Wexler, too, wasn't unconcerned. The producer, in his initial conversation with Hall and Moman, had requested as close to an integrated band as possible—at least have some black players in the horn section. But what with Chalmers's makeshift horn posse, every musician scheduled for the session, save Aretha herself, was white. An incident involving a bunch of Southern white boys was the last thing Wexler needed. What he *did* need was a hit. "Jerry was nervous and tense and unsure of us," Spooner confirms. "It was understandable. Maybe he was just nervous hoping that we would meld with her." Wexler confirms his anxiety: "I took this great singer to Muscle Shoals and mixed her up with this crew of good old boys. I didn't know what the chemistry was going to be. But I settled down once they started playing."

If Wexler tensed at the prospect of a negative reaction from Aretha herself when she saw a dearth of black faces, his fears were allayed by her utter lack of attitude. "Aretha hasn't got the slightest vestige of race attitude," Wexler says. "She is a tremendous promulgator of her race—but there was never anything antiwhite. She didn't care that these boys down there were white. She heard them play!" Indeed, Aretha wasn't yet famous, but she was a pro, and she'd come to Muscle Shoals to work, to record hits. Her demeanor was straightforward, businesslike, and, as was typical for her outside her immediate family and friends, a bit shy.

Dan Penn has perhaps the most vivid recollection of Aretha's arrival at Fame Studios that January afternoon. The fact that Dan is not just a creator and interpreter but an inveterate observer would prove most helpful to a contemporary chronicler of a musical moment almost four decades old. "My little ole mind's eye remembers a really sensitive, polite person—but a pretty confident one," Penn told me thirty-seven years after the fact. "I mean, I think when Jerry Wexler explained to her what he wanted to do, bring her down South, it probably halfway scared her. But I think after she analyzed it, she musta thought, Jerry Wexler—my man. And he's got a plan. And I think when she walked into that room, I think she said, Yup, something's gonna happen. I think she knew just as good as I did sitting over in the corner. I mean, she didn't look like no lamb led to the slaughter. She'd played with all kind of white people. She wasn't upset about the white people, she wasn't upset about the South. I don't think she was upset! She may have been scared to death. But from what I remember, she seemed like kind of a shy person but very confident. I think she had already seen the picture."

The other guys don't necessarily paint such a compelling psychological portrait of the singer when they recall that day, but to the rest of the band, Aretha seemed like a pleasant enough young woman, with an up-to-the-moment hairdo, dressed in an outfit that the delightfully low-key Spooner Oldham amusingly described to me as "dressy-casual." The usual introductions were made, but there was little in the way of a preamble to getting down to business. The atmosphere was professional, and the idea—for everyone present—was to get started right away making music. At this early stage, only Penn sensed that some serious musical throwing-down was afoot: "I didn't know when or how, but I knew lightning was fixin' to flare," Dan says. "I just had that feelin'. She just had this look. Let's just say her aura was lookin' good."

Aretha was accompanied, of course, by her husband-manager, whose aura was significantly less impressive to those assembled. "She came down with her husband, boyfriend, good friend, manager, whatever, Ted White," Hall says. "She's a very quiet woman—never talked at all. Ted did all the talking. He was her husband or whatever—I didn't even get into all that. I just wanted to get down to business."

Clearly, Rick doesn't have the fondest memories of Ted,

for reasons that would emerge over the course of the recording session. Indeed, in most accounts of Aretha during this period, White comes across negatively, and he's routinely characterized as difficult to work with. But decades after White's association with Aretha, it's impossible to do anything more concrete than speculate randomly on the nature of their relationship and Ted's personality at the time. What I can assert, having spoken to White about the making of this record, is that he appears to have mellowed, and as a man in his seventies looks back on this period of his life with a mixture of pride, outrage, wistfulness, and sadness.

Ted White feels wronged by how he's been portrayed in numerous accounts, most famously a notorious 1968 *Time* magazine cover story on his wife that remains one of the most engaging accounts of Aretha's personality but which had nothing but scorn for her husband. Who knows what Ted and Aretha's private relationship was like? It's not for this writer to either condemn or apologize for White (and certainly, with his quasi-warning to me when we spoke— "We're not going to get into a lawsuit situation, are we, Matt?"—I had my guard up), but my impression of the elderly Ted, today, was of a man who wouldn't claim to be a saint but whom circumstances might have compelled, perhaps justifiably, to behave in ways that wouldn't necessarily be seen as particularly endearing or likeable. When White says, "I've been beat up pretty bad by the press previously. I don't want to experience that again," you feel for him, whether you believe he deserved those previous media beatings or not. And it's inarguable that, whatever Ted and Aretha's personal issues, he remains an ardent admirer of his ex-wife's talent. "All I know is she's one of the greatest performers *I've* ever seen," he told me. "She can sing everything from classic to rock-and-roll to gospel to pop. I just think that she's one of the greatest singers that ever lived."

If I sensed an almost pitiable quality in White today, the boys from Muscle Shoals didn't detect it in 1967. In the informal setting of Fame Studios, Ted was dressed up, in a sport coat, perhaps even a full suit. "He was wearing Alabama State Trooper sunglasses," Jimmy Johnson vividly recalls. "You know the kind that's mirrors? And you can't see the eyes? We didn't know what to think. He didn't give us any bad vibe, but he was watching us very closely. And we couldn't see where he was looking. Inside! You could have combed your hair in his lenses."

Contemplation of White's eyewear didn't last very long, however. Aretha would shortly set about casually yet forcefully calling the musicians to attention. Dan Penn, of course, noticed and remembers. "The mechanics of getting ready for the session is takin' place," he says. "And just suddenly, she walks over to the piano, she sits down at the piano stool, and I'm watchin' her. She kinda looks around, like, Nobody's watchin' me. I thought she thought for just a second, Is this not my session? And with all the talent she had, she just hit this unknown chord. Kind of kawunka-kawunka-kawung! Like a bell ringing. And every musician in the room stopped what they were doing, went to their guitars and started tunin' up. They knew someone had come who was gonna cut somethin' heavy on that day. I just thought, Oh, she done stirred 'em up now. This girl at the piano—you were aware that no one could hit that chord. She did it in a very shy way. She didn't do it like, Hey I'm here! It was just her magic."

Peter Guralnick, the first author to chronicle the session in his sublime 1986 book *Sweet Soul Music*, dubbed Aretha's call to action the "magic chord," and few would dispute the designation. Jimmy Johnson says, "We knew when her hands hit the piano that we were in for something really incredible." "She was so cool," David Hood picks up. "She played piano just wonderfully, with great feel—it was this great, gospel-influenced style."

Spooner agrees: "It was probably just a question of testing the piano. She was probably nervous, but you get a grip and you play a note or two and a lot of the tension goes away—on both sides, the player and the listener. And you can determine a lot about a person's potential talent with just a little bit of music."

In 1967, a group of twenty-three-year-olds in rural Alabama was unaccustomed to the experience of a black woman from the North forcefully calling them to attention, in effect, demanding "Respect" at a time when that song still belonged to Otis Redding and when Southern women weren't exactly calling the shots. But from the moment Aretha hit her gospel chord sequence on the piano, the vibe shifted. "The mood was electric," Spooner confirms. "We got down to business essentially right off the bat. There was very little rhetoric. It was all, let's stay with our instruments and get this done." Ted White wasn't surprised by the level of intensity. "You've got Aretha Franklin in the studio," he says. "Expectations are *very* high."

Wexler was the only one who wasn't shaken. "I was too nervous, on edge, apprehensive to be transmogrified," he says today. Furthermore, "I also realized right away how important it was for Aretha to play piano on her own records. I've learned this—this is practically a dictum: If you have a singer who can play, have them play on the record. Good, bad, or indifferent because it brings something to the table that is quintessentially him. I don't care if you play badly, please play." For Aretha to set the tone at the piano, for Jerry, was exactly what was supposed to be happening.

That said, he hadn't been aware of just how gifted a keyboardist Aretha was: "When I heard her play I said, Jesus,
she sounds like Thelonious Monk! I can't believe this."

The futzing around came to an end as the musicians
were initiated into the sound-world of Aretha. "She has
her own harmonic concept, where she can go from blues
to gospel," Wexler says. "She has a very interesting way of
melding, mixing up blues chords and gospel chords,
which throws the musicians off, until they get to learn
the progression. It's almost like Billie Holiday or Frank
Sinatra—you can't keep their time. She's got her own
time, and she goes to inversions that you wouldn't dream
of." The first song on the docket was "I Never Loved a
Man (the Way I Love You)," and Wexler played a basic
demo of the tune over the studio's sound system. It was
the first time the band had heard the song, and the plan
was to record Aretha using head arrangements, meaning
Franklin would take the lead playing piano and singing,
and the other musicians would build their parts around
her. But the initial reaction to this first song was less than
stellar.

"It was an awful, awful demo," Penn says. "We was all
used to good songs. And you had to listen hard to find
anything good about it. It seemed like for a second everybody's spirits kind of dropped: Oh, we gotta cut *that*.

There was a period of silence. Everybody lookin' at each other like, Oh, hell, wish we had us a good song. And then Wexler starts talking, like, 'Come on guys, this is a good song.' He's talking it up and talking it up. Jerry is tryin' to work a little magic of his own, like, 'Hang with me, boys, this is not a bad song.'"

"It was sort of an oddball tune, I thought," Spooner agrees. "Talking about this guy being no good and so forth, a heartbreaker, and a liar and a cheat." Even Ted White concedes that no one liked it: "Nobody cared for it at first. Everybody thought it was too slow, we need an up-tempo." White, however, was partial to the tune, because its composer, Ronnie Shannon, was a recent signee to his Detroit-based management outfit and something of a Ted White discovery. "When I met Ronnie Shannon, I was at a barber shop," White recalls. "Ronnie Shannon came in and asked the barber at the next chair if he could give him the directions to Motown. The guy said, 'Why, are you a singer or something?' He said, 'Well, I'm a singer and a songwriter.' The barber said, 'Why don't you talk to Ted White—he's involved with show business.' So Ronnie waited until the barber finished my hair. We went out to his car and he sang a few songs. In fact, he just came in the night prior to that from Georgia, and he was *staying* in his car. He gave me a few of his songs, sang 'em for me. And I was impressed. I took him back to my building, and we talked about what kind of material I wanted for Aretha. He went up stairs and about two hours later he came down with 'I Never Loved a Man.' "

Shannon became an informal member of Ted and Aretha's Detroit songwriting circle, and when Aretha arrived in Alabama, she had worked out the bones of her vocal arrangements in advance. That was her method: to plan out the basics of her performance and then, once the mics were turned on, to riff at whim. She'd been singing Shannon's "I Never Loved a Man" at home for some time, accompanying herself on a Fender Rhodes, so when she launched into the opening lines—"You're no good, heartbreaker/You're a liar, and you're a cheat/And I don't know why/I let you do these things to me"—her sound was raw and earthy, but the vocal performance itself was polished. Still, there was the question of a full rhythm section arrangement to be dealt with.

Having heard the demo of the song over the speakers, the rhythm section grabbed their instruments and started "doodling," as Spooner calls it. A rough blueprint of the song had been suggested by the recording, and Aretha wasted no time establishing a key. Regular music charts had been eschewed in favor of number charts, rough progressions that could be fitted to any key and standard practice at Fame Studios at the time, as well as Jerry's preferred method of arrangement. "Using the number system, one to seven, you get a series of number indications of the chords and the layout. It's all there," he says. "There's no key indicated, because you can't indicate a key with the number system, like you can with traditional chord writing. But when you've got a song laid out that way, you use your imagination. Somebody picks up a pattern. It's the interstices that you can't arrange—what you do in between." The musicians knew in what general direction the song would head, thanks to the demo and Aretha's initial tempo-and key-setting work at the piano. But a riff, a groove, "the interstices"—what today would largely be deemed the production—was still taking root.

Aside from Ted and Aretha, few were convinced that the song itself was particularly strong, and they weren't clear on how to go about turning what Rick Hall called "a tired blues record" into the hit song for which Aretha and her two Svengalis, White and Wexler, were practically frothing at the mouth.

"But one little guy sittin' over on the electric piano, named Spooner Oldham," Dan Penn recalls of his good and slight-bodied buddy, "out of nowhere, after what seemed like two full minutes of nobody saying a word, here comes Spooner." He starts humming the repeating keyboard pattern that opens the song and around which the record would develop. "The song didn't have a specific meter, really," Spooner said. "So the band just sort of looked at each other like, Well, what do we do? Where do we go now? We were all off in our little worlds trying to figure out a rhythm or a riff. And I just happened to be the one to formulate this little pattern."

"Spooner's got it! Spooner's got it!" Chips cried from his corner of Fame's Studio A, hearing the lick and instantly seizing on its potential to form the groundwork of the track. "I heard Chips, and they all kind of looked at me," Oldham continues. "I just kept playing what I was doing," on the Wurlitzer electric piano. Aretha came in singing the song's assertive, accusing opening line: 'You're no good, heartbreaker.' In the same way that she had called the group to attention less than an hour earlier on the piano, she now did the same, using her other superior instrument—her voice—infusing the song's already direct and provocative opening phrase with a vocal heft and immediacy even the experienced players in the studio were struck by.

"And from there it was like sparkles and shine," Dan Penn says expansively. "After everybody heard her sing, 'You're no good, heartbreaker,' she had five instant fans. I can tell you, she was getting all the respect one person can get from those cats."

"Her piano playing was so good," Hawkins agrees, "that

I just thought, Okay, everything's going to be okay. But what the heck am I gonna play?" Roger, on drums, quickly fell into the groove Spooner and Aretha were laying out. "When she started playing, we all kind of started playing around her," Roger says. "She actually gave you energy. You pick up off of her energy and pick up a part to play very easily." In Roger's case, the developing three-quarter time signature of the song inspired a kind of shuffle—low-key drumming with a solid, centering thwack on the three of each measure. "*Drum* magazine has an article about me," Hawkins told me in his modest, Southern way, "that supposedly I invented the first soul waltz. The song was in three-quarter time, so I just put the cross stick on beat three. I don't really know what made that the first soul waltz. . . ."

With a strong organ part, tight drums, and pumped-up yet simple, propulsive, bluesy bass work from Tommy Cogbill, Aretha opted to hold her acoustic piano entrance for the second verse. "I've got this six-foot baby grand piano—that's all I could afford," Rick says of the instrument. "This little funky piano. We had to drape a quilt over it, because she was singing and playing at the same time." But it wasn't an inferior set of keys that compelled Aretha to hold back; more likely her wide-ranging musical vision, her feel for arrangement, for timing—skills she'd used infrequently or at least mutedly in her recording career up to this point—were responsible for the call. Aretha had observed her Columbia producers' procedures, and was now able, for the first time, to marry what she'd picked up over six years in the studio to her keen natural musicality. "I don't know whose idea it was to save Aretha's piano for the second verse. I know *I* didn't say, 'You lay out,'" Spooner says today with a laugh. "I think it just sort of happened. She was playing great. My guess is she started singing along with me and she chose to play piano where she did. That was her arrangement and her artistic thing coming."

With the rhythm track thus arranged, Wexler turned his attention to Charlie Chalmers, leader of the horn section. "Charlie has got the horns way back in the corner of the studio," Wex remembers. "While we're running a track, I said, 'Charlie, let's figure out the horn parts.'"

"I got 'em," Charlie replied.

While Aretha, Spooner, Tommy, and Roger, along with guitarists Johnson and Moman, were working out the rhythm part, Charlie had been quietly shuttling back and forth from the studio proper, where he would seize on bits and pieces of the burgeoning arrangement, and a small office upstairs, where he was rapidly writing out horn charts for his players, assembled willy-nilly entirely for their ability to read such notation.

"I wrote the charts out as Aretha was working up the

song with the rhythm players," Charlie told me, still proud years later of having been able to crank out such a polished, powerful chart so quickly. "I got out my manuscript paper, and I just started writing out some parts, some unison parts first, then we added the harmonies, kind of broke out on harmonies on the second pass. I just kind of sat there and jotted 'em out."

"It was real quick," Spooner confirms. "I don't know if he wrote 'em down or dreamed 'em up, but it was just right there, right now. It was wonderful in terms of the spontaneity of everyone, the creativity."

The horn arrangement on "I Never Loved a Man" is stellar, particularly effective during the breakdown section of the song's chorus, when all instruments fall out, except for Aretha and her own overdubbed background vocal, until a powerful brass blast brings the players back in.

"That break in there is out of time," Chips explains. "But it felt right. We were going over and over and over with that particular part of that song. Tommy Cogbill and I worked that part out and put that odd break in it. I was making changes in the song and Aretha would just go right to what I was doing. She's really talented. I mean she is *really* talented."

Talented enough that the process of cutting "I Never Loved a Man (the Way I Love You)" took just a few hours and three, maybe four takes, by all remembrances. Everyone in the studio—save Aretha—was stunned. Wexler had to restrain himself from contacting radio DJs on the spot to start promoting his latest "find." "Ooh, it was good. It was real good," Jerry says emphatically of the playback. "We didn't necessarily think we had a global monster, but we all felt very good."

"Blown away" is the phrase most often used by the guys who were on the floor, when they spoke to me about the session. "When we finished it, I loved it," Chips says. "Aretha is an artist." "Oh, it was killer," Chalmers agrees. "I mean, she lays such a groove down. She brings the best out of you. It was incredible. And I was just really thrilled that we pulled it off without the regular players!" "She sung her heart out, played piano," Rick Hall says, seemingly still impressed. "I mean, she was *it*. Everything else, all the other players, was just icing on the cake."

In his book *The World of Soul*, rhythm-and-blues authority Arnold Shaw writes of "I Never Loved a Man," "Aretha cut—literally delivered herself of—one of the most perfect soul disks ever made. . . . The record has the rare quality of leaving you before you are ready to leave it." I listened to the track literally hundreds of times over the course of writing about Aretha, and, as Shaw suggests, I'm still not ready to leave the song. What's at once striking is how almost radically different the sheer quality of Aretha's voice sounds from even her recent Columbia work. The first song Aretha recorded for that label was "Today I Sing the Blues," and it's notable that with "I Never Loved a Man," the singer once again inaugurated her relationship with a new company with a sophisticated, modern blues tune. But almost overnight her voice, though it was always knowing and full of feeling, had gained in heft, had lost its girlish brightness and acquired a kind of smoky brilliancy. Was it the new, more personal material, or something as mundane as an increase in Aretha's cigarette habit? In the space of one three-minute song, Franklin graduated from singer to artist.

From the opening couplet Aretha sounds utterly in control of her voice, at once pleading, intense and yet playful, sexy. The singer has superb natural technique: There never appears to be labor involved in her vocal performance; rather she seems to get out of the way of her singing, letting the vocal lines ride on her breath, letting her breath do the work for her, as if the singing is literally spinning out of her mouth on a well-calibrated release of air. It's that kind of control that allows her to slide into a phrase like "My friends keep telling me/that you ain't no good," bending the word "friends" at once bluesily and prettily, and then leap into pure gospel release on the "But oh-oh-ohhh" that follows.

"I Never Loved a Man" is characterized throughout by

this push-pull of intensity and calm. The Wurlitzer pattern, haunting, almost eerie, and yet grounding for the listener, is rooted in the blues tradition of repetition. As Spooner says, there's motion to the song, and as Aretha carefully builds her vocal, as her piano kicks in and the thrust of her "polished gospel" (in Hawkins's words) keyboard style intensifies, and as the horn blasts increase in frequency and power, one feels as if one is being led, taken toward some inevitable climax, which arrives, surprisingly, when the instrumentation disappears entirely, the time signature changes, and Aretha sings, her voice doubled, "Loved a man/the way that I/I love you." The groove of the track literally seizes the listener from the opening bar and doesn't let up except during those a cappella breakdowns, which come as almost a relief, Aretha seemingly stamping out a rising tide of groove that's under her control alone. Everything about the song, from the interplay of instruments, to the developing pitch, to Aretha's raw yet beautiful singing, is organic.

Thirty-seven years after the song was recorded, Jerry Wexler and I sat in his home office in East Hampton and listened to it. "This track has such a groove!" he said seconds into the song. "I Never Loved a Man" was the song he would show the most enthusiasm for as we listened to the entire album track by track. "The hero of that record is Spooner Oldham. The way his Wurlitzer interfaced with her acoustic piano. You know, that's the moment for me. The moment that it's happening in the studio. Not the playback, not the gold record, not the charts. The moment when that good take is happening—that's my euphoria."

seven

"The Incident"

One of the high points of Aretha Franklin's 1972 *Amazing Grace* album, which, along with *I Never Loved a Man the Way I Love You*, is one of the peaks of her career, is a song called "Precious Memories," performed as a duet with the Reverend James Cleveland, her musical tutor from years before. "Precious memories, how they linger," the gospel standard goes. "How they ever flood my soul. In the stillness of the midnight, sacred scenes unfold." Aretha's own memories of the recording of "I Never Loved a Man," or at least of the turmoil that ensued, are somewhat vague ("It's been so long and so many things have happened since those days, I really don't recall," she says of her January 24, 1967 stint in the South), but the sacred scene is undeniably precious to her ("It made her a star!" David Ritz says. "And she loved being a star."). The question of memory—how it selects, enhances, edits, elides, and, often, fails—is unavoidable in a chronicle of the making of *I Never Loved a Man*, especially when it comes to what was alternately described to me as "the incident," "the ruckus," "the scuffle," "the skirmish," "the fracas," "the contretemps" (this last term from Jerry Wexler, of course). Many of the people who were present claim not to remember what happened in the studio as work on the first cut neared completion. Some genuinely don't recall, and others would simply prefer to forget. One assumes still others relish the legend that continues to surround Aretha's inaugural Atlantic outing, as it somehow elevates the making of a pop record to the realm of myth.

"I don't think people want to really tell the whole story," Charlie Chalmers says with some understatement. And those who are forthcoming give inconsistent renderings. What I discovered trying to suss out and piece together the legend of this session's sudden turn for the worse—and what I perhaps should have realized all along—was that "the misunderstanding," though it had repercussions for some of the players in this story and foretold of future events for others, was fundamentally irrelevant, or at least is in retrospect. As David Hood told me, "The story has become bigger than the actual happening." *I Never Loved a Man the Way I Love You*, of course, got made. Ultimately, that's what matters. A lurid retelling of the tale thirty-seven

years later? Gossipy and immaterial. And yet, as the fin-
ishing touches were put on "I Never Loved a Man," it started
to look as if *I Never Loved a Man* might not happen. And
so . . .

With one monster track in the can, a celebration was in
order. Problem was, in 1967, Colbert was still a dry county;
if any drinking were to go down, it would happen surrepti-
tiously, with bottles smuggled into the studio from elsewhere. Rick didn't allow drinking on a session, and the
players he employed weren't about to go against his strin-
gent, iron-fist-enforced rules. "Anyone who worked for
Rick would *never* have done that in a million years," Jimmy
Johnson says of drinking on the job.

Fame may have adopted a policy of prohibition in keeping with the local laws, but, as Dan Penn straightfor-
wardly asserts, "Drinking and music went together." It was
outlawed in the studio, but that didn't mean it didn't happen. One could argue that it's the rare rock-music session
that *doesn't* involve some kind of perspective-altering or
inhibition-relaxing agent. And, of course, while excessive
imbibing can derail a musical endeavor, when musicians
do lube themselves up with a shot of Jack Daniels, a couple of tall boys, a slug of vodka straight out of the bottle,
the result is often a funky, sensitive, powerhouse recording. In the name of professionalism, Hall would logically
insist on a dry establishment, but it was an open secret, to

some degree, that among certain players drinking would and did go on. If the presence of booze had its pluses and minuses in the recording world, in a relationship it could prove similarly problematic, as Aretha herself well knew: "Alcohol played a destructive role," she writes of her marriage to Ted. "Drinking ultimately damaged, and finally destroyed, our relationship." According to numerous published accounts, anecdotes relayed to me off the record, and to Aretha herself, drinking was a prominent element in the troubled Franklin/White marriage, and it would carry over to this moment in their professional lives, at Muscle Shoals.

But at least the couple arrived at the session sober (and, indeed, by all accounts, Aretha herself stayed that way). The same cannot be said, allegedly, for the trumpet player from Memphis, whose very presence on the scene confounded all the others. Not a lot was or is known about Ken Laxton, the trumpet player who has not been named in previous accounts of this session. It didn't take much sleuthing to determine the identity of the phantom trumpeter who triggered the unraveling of the session: A quick look at the liner notes of the current Rhino Records reissue of *I Never Loved a Man* indicates that there was a lone trumpet player on the title track, and that musician is not credited on any other song on the album. That player is Ken Laxton, whom I was unable to track down during my research, despite considerable, time-consuming efforts. Apparently, Laxton ended up as an engineer on recording sessions in Nashville, though the Nashville Music Commission has no record of his work or whereabouts. Rumor has it that he also worked for a time as a barber. By most accounts, he was a talented trumpeter. But personality-wise, according to the people I spoke with, he could sometimes rub folks the wrong way.

"He was a little bit mouthy," says Chalmers, the man who hired him. "Thought he was the hippest thing in the world. I knew his attitude, but I hired him because I knew he could cut a reading gig. But he had kind of a be-bop, jive attitude." Moman had encountered him briefly as well, back in Memphis. "He's alright, but he always would stir up trouble," Chips told me. "He was just always kind of smart about things, kind of a smart-aleck guy."

A difficult personality was one thing; a difficult personality plus alcohol was another. "He was a little inebriated," Johnson recalls. "We didn't know him. He was like a foreign person—actually a good trumpet player. But he stupidly drank! He was drinking when he got there."

Arranging and recording "I Never Loved a Man" went remarkably swiftly, but there was nevertheless downtime for the musicians on the floor, particularly for the horn players, who spent much of the afternoon lounging on the couch against a back wall of the studio as Chalmers worked out their parts upstairs. For a buzzing guy with an unpredictable temperament, such lulls would provide the perfect opportunity to stir up trouble. No one disputes the suggestion that Laxton began behaving inappropriately toward Aretha.

"The word we got was that he kind of got a little—let's not say totally out of line, but he got a little friendly with Aretha," Johnson says. "He was sayin', 'Aretha, baby.' You know, just somethin' you don't do, respectin' an artist." The fact that Laxton was a Memphis musician, and not a local, perhaps fueled any brewing misunderstanding. "In Memphis, the scene was a little more hip—the musicians, white and black, would hang out together and kid with each other," Hood explains. "And I think he was thinking he was being cute and kidding. And he made some remarks that didn't go down so well with Aretha, or at least didn't go down so well with Ted. I don't think he was trying to start anything, or be fresh necessarily. But it was taken the wrong way: a white musician talking very familiar with Aretha with her husband there."

"I always heard he patted her on the butt or somethin'," Penn picks up. "And what would have been wrong with that anyway?"

Whether there was flirting, vulgar talk, or actual butt-patting, Ted White witnessed something and took offense.

"There were a few remarks made," White told me. "He made a remark about Aretha, something about Aretha that was derogatory. And it offended me, and I reacted to it. I asked Jerry to get rid of the guy." Not before, however, White himself had unpredictably (and briefly, it would turn out) befriended the offender. "They were drinking out of the same bottle," Wexler recalled in his autobiography. "A redneck patronizing a black man is a dangerous camaraderie." "Palship turned into a kind of alcoholic hostility," Wexler further remembered for an interviewer. Today, at eighty-seven, Jerry doesn't have quite as vivid a recall of the proceedings as he did at seventy-five, when he wrote his book. But Peter Guralnick's account of the day, in *Sweet Soul Music*, corroborates Wex's version of events. The way Ted White neatly tells it, however, a wayward trumpeter got out of line, White called him on it, and the matter was resolved.

Everyone agrees on that much, more or less, but the story is murky. When I spoke to him, White was reluctant to get into the details of that afternoon at Fame, perhaps to avoid addressing Hall's and Wexler's claim that he, like Laxton, was drunk, or at least close to it. "Ted starts drinking," Hall alleges. "He's on the floor with the musicians. I'm in the control room with Jerry. I don't recall if it's gin or vodka, but by this time he's drinking pretty good. Everyone's starting to get tense. I can't drink, 'cause I'm engineering. Wex can't drink because he's got his balls on the line. Everyone's uptight, except Ted. Well, shortly, he comes into the control room and says, 'Jerry, I want the trumpet player fired.' Jerry says, 'Why?' Ted says, 'He's making passes at Aretha.' I think his exact words were"— and here Hall adopts a kind of sultry-sinister tone—" 'He's got eyes for Aretha.'"

Almost every time I asked for an interview subject's impressions of Ted, the immediate response was, "Turn off your tape recorder." White apparently came across as an intense and controlling figure, though the musicians concede he was a complicated person and was personable enough on this and future sessions; he could even be called, on occasion, a nice guy. Jimmy Johnson recalls the gift of a watch at Christmastime—Ted's idea—with the words "Respectfully, Aretha" inscribed on it. But most of the people I interviewed were unable to view the man with anything other than mistrust, frustration, and anger. No one can know the exact nature of this marriage as it existed on its own private terms (Aretha caustically called her years with White "a learning experience"), but the players on *I Never Loved a Man* had their impressions and convictions; for propriety's sake and perhaps out of fear of reprisal—and largely out of respect for Aretha—they declined to offer them on the record. "I'd hate for Aretha to get mad at me," one musician demurred, even though he hadn't been in contact with the singer for almost thirty years.

Despite such unflattering portrayals, somehow I felt for Ted White, who, though he never admitted to any kind of misbehavior over the course of our conversation, nevertheless, speaks of this period of his life in a kind of penitential tone. He's palpably uncomfortable discussing working with his ex-wife, and when he says softly, "It's forty years ago. Let it bury itself," it's nothing as much as sad.

To be fair, the idea of repairing to a backwoods town in the deep South couldn't and didn't put White at ease. "Oh, there was serious tension," White told me, "because I was in Muscle Shoals, Alabama, in 1967. It *wasn't* a relaxed situation." With even the least experienced of the musicians accustomed to working with black artists, they could recognize and understand his discomfort. "I think Ted was paranoid—coming to the South," Johnson says evenly. "I imagine it was hard to come down South to cut a record." David Hood agrees: "There were never any racial problems with us, at least in the music community around here. But there was nobody black [on the session] except Aretha and Ted. That was a time when you would notice something like that."

An angry, possibly intoxicated husband and an uppity, definitely intoxicated horn player were the last things

Rick Hall needed. He had been anxious to begin with, partly with the specter of another significant and potentially career-making (or -breaking) Atlantic session, partly because of the changes to Fame's setup that Wexler and his brilliant New York engineer, Tom Dowd, had insisted on. "I brought Wilson Pickett to Muscle Shoals before I brought Aretha, and all Rick had was mono," Wexler told me. "I said, Rick, I'm bringing Aretha Franklin—I need at least four tracks. It broke his heart, but he put in a three-track." That was still considerably more low-tech than the Ampex eight-track recorder Dowd had the foresight to encourage Wexler to procure almost a decade earlier. "Les Paul and Mary Ford had the first eight-track," Wexler recalls of the pioneering guitarist and his wife. "Tommy Dowd bought us the third. We were the first record company to have real multiples, years before anybody else." Atlantic's New York studio was state-of-the-art at the time, but Fame was still decidedly old-school.

The studio had been monaural at the time of the Pickett sessions, meaning, essentially, that the mics were turned on and the song as played was the song on the recording, with no possibility for overdubs. For Aretha's session, mono wouldn't do, and so Wexler successfully pressed Hall to install more tracks. The equipment, however, was still fairly new to him, and Dowd's instruction—despite the man's famously affable air—was agitating to Rick. Everyone loved Tom Dowd, the onetime physicist who had worked on the Manhattan Project before getting involved in the music business (perhaps the perfect preparation for a career alongside Wexler and Ertegun). But no one could have given Hall engineering input that would have been received appreciatively at the time.

"I was a nervous wreck," Hall confirmed. "Wexler was standing over my shoulder while I'm engineering, and Tom Dowd was sitting there, and between the two of them—the directions I was getting: turn him up, turn him down, wait a minute, you're losing the singer. . . ."

"I remember lookin' up at the glass and seeing Rick, with Tom Dowd over his shoulder, showin' him the new way to do it," Dan Penn remembers. "You know, Rick Hall is a smart cat, but he does things by method. Once he learns somethin', that's the way he do it. So here's a man from New York, standing over his shoulder saying, 'No, don't do it that way—turn it to the left, turn it to the right.' Rick's cutting this big smash record—probably don't know it at that point but part of him does—but what was on his mind was, What are these Yankees doin', tearing up my studio? That's what I think Rick had on his mind at least part of the day. And that'll make you drink when you're Southern."

For a while, Rick held off. But White's rising agitation

and Wex's instruction that he fire the restive trumpeter started to push Rick past his limits. "They both had had a few drinks," Hall told me of White and Laxton. "This guy made some remarks. Ted's getting a little drunker. It's six P.M., seven P.M.—we haven't eaten . . ." If Laxton were out of line, White wasn't exactly the type to let the affront slide. Between the two of them, plus a nerved-up Wex in the control booth, Rick was increasingly overwhelmed. At Jerry's commission, a deflated Hall confronted Laxton, axing him after the final take. Evening was upon them, one undeniably great track had been recorded, but nerves were fraying: It seemed as good a time as any to take a break and cool off before moving on to the next song, which had only just been introduced onto the schedule.

"I was always a hanger-oner," Dan Penn told me in his simultaneously self-deprecating and forceful way. "Just hang around long enough, somethin' will rub off on you, you know?" That ethos—along with his preexisting awareness of Aretha's talent—is what compelled Dan to travel to Muscle Shoals for the session, and to make sure he brought his latest composition, written with Chips, along with him. "Me and Chips talked about it," Penn says now. "I brought up the fact that this girl Wexler was cutting was going to be pretty heavy, and maybe we ought to play 'Do Right' for Jerry." Up in Memphis, prior to the Franklin gig, Dan and

Chips threw together a rough demo of "Do Right Woman— Do Right Man," in the hopes of persuading Wex—and Ree—to record the song. It worked. Wexler loved the tune, though he recognized at once that it was unfinished and in need of a bridge.

As Laxton's hepcat insouciance turned ugly; as Rick and Jerry bickered in the booth; as Ted (allegedly) started partying on the studio floor; and as Aretha nailed each vocal take of "I Never Loved a Man," taking the performance to a higher level with each run-through, Dan was hiding out in a tiny room adjacent to Rick's office, trying to devise a bridge for his song.

Penn recalls the process of working out the number, as he does so slipping into Jerry's accent, affecting a high, girlish register to impersonate Aretha, and using his own beautiful, soul-drenched voice to sing certain phrases from the song. "Jerry came up to me and said, 'I love the song, man. I really dig the song—we're gonna cut it. But it doesn't have any words for the bridge.' I said, 'You're gonna cut it? We'll have words before the day is out.' So I go out to the cloak closet, under the stairs where you go up to Rick's office—it's kind of a little spot where you can get by yourself. And so I went in there, and I'm tryin' to work on the song. I get to, 'They say it's a man's world' and I'm stuck for a second. And all of a sudden Jerry peeps his head in the door and says, 'Have you got it? Have you got it?' I said,

'This is what I've got, Jerry: "They say it's a man's world."' And he says, 'Oh, I've got the next part: "But you can't prove that by me."' I said, 'Terrific.' I wrote that down—I'll take it. So now I'm goin', 'They say it's a man's world but you can't prove that by me.' 'Bout that time Aretha stuck her head in and she said, 'Dan, are you about got it?' I said, 'This is what I've got, Aretha: "They say it's a man's world, but you can't prove that by me."' She said, 'Oh, I have the next part.' I said, 'What is that?' She said, '"As long as we're together baby, show some respect for me."' I said, 'I'll take that.' I wrote it down. And it worked! They actually helped write the words to that song."

The bridge, and thus the song, was completed at roughly the same time as "I Never Loved a Man" finished tracking. Most of the musicians left to get food. Ted White, still enraged by Laxton's forwardness with his wife, went back to the hotel, the Downtowner Motor Inn, in Florence. "Four stories—the biggest in town," Jimmy Johnson jokes of the place.

Johnson traces the start of Rick's hitting the bottle to a minicelebration back in Wexler's room in the motel. "Jerry and Rick are in Wexler's room toastin'," Jimmy recounts. "Having a little scotch, getting a little tipsy. Which is fine! Heck, they deserved it. Well, phone rings—this is how I heard it—Wexler takes the call, and he's informed by Ted White that he'll be leaving in the morning, heading back to New York, he ain't gonna put up with this shit. And Wexler, very cool guy that he is, just says, 'Don't talk to me, talk to my lawyer.' That's all he said. And he hangs up the phone and he tells Rick. Well, Rick sees it going down the tube and decides to mediate. He only wanted to smooth it over—he tried to salvage what was going down, but he shouldn't have done it tipsy. They get into a heated argument, and instead of smoothing it over, he stirred the shit. I'm sure he didn't mean to. Rick Hall's basically a nice guy. But he was trying to help things, and you can't do it when you're not sober."

Jimmy recalls events thirty-some-odd years old with an air of authority, and this rendering of things certainly makes for a compelling story. Unfortunately, it's utter hearsay, as, by his own admission, Johnson wasn't there. Rick Hall, however, was, and he told me that he didn't wait for any kind of party back at the hotel to pour himself a cocktail. And when he did start drinking, still at Fame Studios, it was out of despair, not celebration: Rick denies the reaction to "I Never Loved a Man" was quite as ecstatic as the others present recall. "I didn't think we had shit," he says succinctly. Whether it was in answer to Laxton's actions—and, at the risk of sounding histrionic, if the trumpeter did in fact touch Aretha or spoke to her suggestively, it amounts to sexual harassment of a major woman artist in an environment in which she largely should have been calling the shots—or because he wanted to make amends for what he perceived to be a failed session, Hall took it upon himself to pursue White and right the day's wrongs.

"We thought it was a horrible day," Rick continues. "I felt so defeated at the end of the day. I thought, we had this big shot and we blew it. I tell Jerry I'm depressed, so I have a drink. I said, 'I'm going to the hotel, make peace.' Wex says, 'No, Rick. I'll take care of it.' I say, 'No, I'm going.' Fifteen minutes later, Ted and I are in a knock-down, drag-out. We both had had drinks. My intentions are good, but he's still bitter about the day. He's talking about, 'Motherfucking redneck bunch of hillbillies. Shut up, you ignorant hick.' And I say, 'You gonna "redneck" me one more time, gonna "whitey" me one more time, and I'm gonna "nigger" you.' And bam!"

Rick demurs from going any further with his story. He followed White to the hotel to repair the day's damage, and there was an altercation. Period. Was there a hotel-room party in full swing, at which he was at the center? "Thank goodness, I went to bed—I didn't go," Charlie Chalmers said as our conversation veered toward "the incident," but before I'd asked a single question about it. Didn't go? "To the party, to the hotel." At that point Charlie stopped short, as if wary of heading into dangerous terrain. No one wants to step on toes, make accusations, especially ones for which they have little or no proof. This is a remarkably laid-back, unassuming group of people, with a few exceptions. Ted White seemed volatile, the trumpet player was an asshole, and Rick Hall showed poor judgment. Essentially, that's what Aretha Franklin's Muscle Shoals debacle boiled down to. Wexler, in his book, calls the scene at the hotel, "*Walpurgisnacht,* a Wagnerian shit storm," and remembers voices raised, doors slammed, and, he told an interviewer, possibly gunshots. This last detail is may be an instance of Wexler mugging, heightening the drama of the situation as a PR move of sorts. There was certainly the possibility for violence inherent in the assemblage that day, and it's possible the friction was far worse, even, than the vivid rumors and hearsay suggest. It seems unlikely, however, that shots were fired at the Downtowner Motor Inn, considering no police were called to the scene. The potential was certainly there, bubbling under. As Ted White says, he was in Muscle Shoals, Alabama, in 1967—there was tension. But the tension, the eruption, the coming-to-blows, whether grounded in the truth, an utter fabrication, or somewhere in between (the most likely scenario) is today somewhat fantastical, and succeeds more in crafting a sturdy, durable sort of lore that remains attached to Aretha's early Atlantic work, than it does in illuminating the characters of the key players. The artistic process—Aretha's genius—was completely apart from any "fracas," "skirmish," or "contretemps." Aretha was there to make music.

Music-making was what was still happening back at Fame when most of the dramatis personae had moved on to the hotel. The horn section dispersed, Ted fled, Rick followed, with Wex in hot pursuit. Meanwhile, Dan, Chips, Spooner, Tommy Cogbill, and Aretha kept their focus and set to work laying down "Do Right Woman." "There wasn't nobody there but the four of us," Chips remembers. "While they were gone, we was just not going to sit at the studio and do nothing. So we just turned everything on and started recording. They were having that big fight. We were trying to finish the song, and we just put it down. We got her key and we put it down."

They laid down tracks in Aretha's key, but they didn't get her vocal. She'd only just heard the song for the first time a few hours earlier, and was apprehensive about tackling the number with tape rolling. She grasped the melody and had a handle on the chords, but she couldn't quite pin down the feel of the piece. And for Aretha, the vibe of a song, the feeling it evoked in her, was the crucial ingredient of her performance. "If I can't feel it, I can't sing it," she has said. And at this particular moment, she wasn't feeling it.

"She liked the song but hadn't had time to practice it or

settle into it," Spooner confirms. "I remember there was Roger playing the drums and Cogbill playing the bass. And I'm on these little simplistic chords on organ, just holding chords so the song would be understood. And that was sort of where it was left. Dan had to sing the vocal, because she didn't know the song, in the wrong key for him. That's what they left with—Dan singing the wrong-key vocal and this little simplistic organ and a bass and a drum. We had a whole week to do everything—we had plenty of time—so there was no hurry to do anything in particular." (The notion that a week was more than enough time to record an entire album seems hilarious by today's slicker standards.)

"She didn't just jump on songs, you know," Dan continues. "So I had to do the track in her key. I had to sing real high. And back then I didn't really care—I'd try anything. But as I remember, I went home that night and I was so dejected. I thought—you ain't gonna make any money on that, kid. Because all it was, was Cogbill going bum-bum, and Spooner had his little organ holdin' there, and me screaming at the top of my voice—it sounded pitiful."

Still, as Spooner says, there would be plenty of time to turn the rough track into something substantial. "I went home and went to bed and thought everything was fine," says Spooner. "I was excited to be there the next morning, because I knew one thing in my head: no matter what any-body was gonna come in saying, I knew we were off to a good start. I thought it was a good day and I wasn't going to accept anything less than that."

No one knew that back at the hotel irreparable rifts were forming. It occurred to no one that there would be no further recording the following day, that the session would be abruptly canceled.

"I came to work at ten o'clock the next morning as scheduled," Spooner continues. "And I remember the jan-itor was the only person I could find. And I said finally, 'I wonder where everyone is—I think we got a session today.' He says, 'I think they've called it off.' No one told me not to come. I was there to work."

"When we came to work the next day, Rick's car is sittin' out in front," Jimmy Johnson asserts. "The door to the building is locked. We can't get in! So we're standing out there for about an hour. He finally comes to the door, and looks like he's hung over. He hadn't had any sleep. I'm sure he was in despair. And he said, 'There'll be no session today.' And we're like, why? And he wouldn't tell us. Things were kept away from us. We always felt like pawns. It was just, Work from the shoulders down, boys."

They didn't know that Jerry, in an instant, had severed all ties to Rick: "How could you do that?" he'd berated the younger man. "We had everything going so good. I begged you not to drink." They didn't know that Ted and Aretha had presumably gotten into an argument of their own, that Aretha had fled the hotel and called Wex late at night from a diner down the road, sounding upset. They didn't know that Aretha and Ted would separately go straight to the airport the next morning, perversely running into each other there, as Franklin remembers it. Later, they'd hear stories and draw conclusions. "I blame it on the liquor," Chips says today. "I think it started—and a lot of things start like this—when people drink out of the other person's bottle. After three or four drinks, then it really ain't no one's fault. It's the liquor. I was surprised 'cause we had a great song cut. I couldn't imagine a little skirmish would stop the session." He pauses, before continuing. "I always thought that Rick and Aretha's husband ought to get together and whup Ken Laxton. That's what they oughta done."

"Do Right Woman" was incomplete—no B-side for "I Never Loved a Man." And there were plenty of other songs that needed to be recorded before Aretha had a full album. Weeks later, Jerry Wexler, that virtual oracle of the record industry, would figure out a way to rescue the project, would track down Aretha after two solid weeks following her flight from Florence, during which she'd apparently fallen off the face of the earth, and would get the Muscle Shoals boys back to work on Aretha's music. But on January

25, twenty-four hours after Aretha had arrived at Fame, Wex had one great song but no B-side, and his recent label acquisition, the woman he was starting to suspect might be able to deliver the hits he craved, was missing. For the time being at least, Aretha had disappeared. He packed up and returned to New York that day as well.

No one told the players what was up. Session cancelled—that's all they heard. Spooner, for one, was confused but unfazed. Rick gave them no details, shut down completely on the subject of the blow-up, merely expected them at work for the next scheduled session—no questions asked. But that was fine by Spooner. "Way I do things, I never ask," Spooner told me, exemplifying the go-with-the-flow Southern charm that all the Muscle Shoals musicians possess. "Everyone else does, so I get it like third-hand, and that's always good enough for me. I get everybody's interpretation, and I just keep goin' on livin'."

eight

A Newfound Respect

For two weeks, Wexler spun in place trying to find Aretha. He tried reaching her at home in New York— no luck. He called the Detroit residence, to no avail. He tried her father's church, New Bethel Baptist, but no one had any leads on Aretha's whereabouts. He was beside himself, in anguish over the rocky denouement of the brief stint in Muscle Shoals. But the executive in him was angry. He was desperate to get Aretha back into the studio and mortified about the way his bright idea to go down South had withered, but a contract had nevertheless been signed and money had changed hands. Whether by personal pleading or legal recourse, he *would* get Aretha Franklin back in the studio. And this time he would do so in New York, at Atlantic's own facility, without the contrarian presence of Rick Hall, in a venue where Ted White could be consigned to the sidelines, and where Wexler himself would be commandingly, unequivocally in charge.

There was no climactic moment to Wexler's detective work, however, no point at which Aretha was at last dramatically discovered in hiding, after weeks of furious investigation. No, after cooling off for a couple of weeks, in Detroit according to White, Aretha simply reappeared, telephoning Wexler, ready to resume work on her album. They didn't discuss what had occurred in Alabama; they avoided the topic of Aretha's incommunicado state. Both were embarrassed by the outcome of the trip to Muscle Shoals, and happy not to discuss it. They merely agreed to pick up where they had left off as soon as possible, slating a time for Aretha to come in and lay down the vocal for "Do Right Woman," the song that had been abandoned in the South. For other tracks, a backing band would have to be hastily assembled: Jerry still wanted to use the Fame players, and he began concocting a scheme to bring them north.

He needed to act quickly to get both Aretha and the other musicians to continue recording: Upon returning to New York, he'd printed acetates of "I Never Loved a Man" and leaked them to DJs. The response was spectacular: Everyone was eager to add the song to their play lists as soon as possible. Louise Bishop was one such DJ: "Jerry called me and played about eight bars of the test pressing of 'I Never Loved a Man,' " she remembers. "I told him to stop it. And he said, 'Why stop it?' I said, 'It's a hit.' He said, 'You didn't hear it all!' I said, 'I don't need to! I know what Aretha can do with the rest. I have that feeling.' She drove it home." The record was a guaranteed smash, but it had no B-side.

Wexler would devise a ruse to lure the Muscle Shoals gang to New York. He was aware he couldn't let Hall know that he planned to continue cutting the album using Rick's players but without Rick's involvement. That would put the boys in too awkward a situation—they were already uneasy around Rick, and he didn't intend to make things any worse for them. Wex could afford a rift with Hall; the rapid disintegration of his musical love affair with Fame was a disappointment, but it would have little day-to-day impact on Jerry professionally. In fact, Jerry was more livid than he was disappointed, and for his own sake felt no compunction about testing the loyalty of Hall's rhythm section. Today, white-bearded Jerry cultivates for himself an image as what one observer calls "the Santa Claus of R&B," and he is without a doubt a deservedly beloved elder statesman of the genre, but in his business dealings he was notoriously ruthless, by many accounts a terror to deal with. In the wake of Muscle Shoals he practically welcomed a battle with Fame's owner. Spooner, Jimmy, and Roger, however, depended on Rick for their livelihood.

But to back a different artist, someone other than Aretha—that was an assignment the Fame rhythm section could accept with little fear of reprisal.

King Curtis, real name Curtis Ousley, was a spectacular tenor saxophone player, who in those years had become a core figure on the Atlantic force after stints at Capitol and other labels, where he provided brass backup for various artists as well as releasing his own solo material. Curtis would chart several instrumental (in both senses of the word) top-forty hits in the sixties, a rare feat for that era as now, including "Soul Twist" and "Soul Serenade," a number that would make its way, with a vocal part added, onto Aretha's album as well. Wexler adored the gregarious, multitalented musician, arranger, bandleader and producer (as did most everyone else in the music business), calling him an "integral conveyor of the Atlantic sound." Why not bring up the crew of funky Southerners to play on a King Curtis record and subsequently, secretly, on Aretha's?

Jerry got on the phone, not to Rick, but to his band. "I got a call: 'Would you come to New York?'" Spooner remembers. "Well, sure, surely. I never asked Rick. The way I work is—I'm signed as a songwriter, but I'm not signed to play exclusive. In other words, first come first served."

Jimmy Johnson was awed to have gotten the call from the man himself. "First phone call I ever got from him," he says today. "I could hardly speak. I mean, his voice is so unbelievably commanding. 'Jimmy! How ya doin'? You wanna come to New York and play on a King Curtis session?' For him to call me at home—if John Kennedy had called me it wouldn't have meant shit next to that. He really wanted us to come up to do the Aretha album, but he knew that if Rick heard we was cutting Aretha. . . . So we cut an album called *King Curtis Plays the Great Memphis Hits*. But that was just a smokescreen. But we didn't know that at the time! So the last day—we're fixing to leave the next day—Jerry says, 'Guys, can I have a meeting? It looks like Aretha's record that you just cut is a hit.' We were freaked out. And he said, 'Could you guys stay over two or three more days and we'll finish her album?' That's what we *really* were called for. Even then it didn't hit us! Rick would have tried to stop us. He was coproducer on the first two Aretha sides, and he would want us to stand by him. It would have put a real big strain on us and him. So I'm glad they did it the way they did it."

To secure the other players required no dissembling. Charlie Chalmers was only too happy to come up and play, especially with King Curtis. "Curtis and I always just had a great time. We would cut up so bad that Tom Dowd would have to tell us, 'Hey, guys, we're trying to cut a record here.' We just constantly had each other laughing and carrying on." That kind of levity was exactly the element Wexler sought to introduce into the session after the friction of a few weeks before. The fact that Curtis was black, he was sure, would also make the vibe more appealing for Aretha. With her sisters, Erma and Carolyn, and Cissy Houston invited to sing backup, and with trumpeter Ernie Royal and baritone sax player Willie Bridges joining Curtis in the horn section, the racial split among the musicians was much more even than it had been at Fame.

Hearing that fellow Memphians Cogbill and Moman would be joining the others in New York, Dan Penn, naturally, decided to tag along. He recalls showing up at Atlantic's impressive studio with its massive, glassed-in control booth for day one. "Wexler didn't waste any breath," Penn says. "As soon as he said hello to everybody, he said, Dan, you and Chips come with me. He took us into the control room and he played Aretha's 'Do Right Woman,' that she'd played piano and her sisters had sang on. It was just amazing, like miraculous that this had been done. And I really thought, on that day, that that was the best record I ever heard. Not just cause it was my song—I just liked the record. It was beautiful. I still wonder what kind of talent it takes to pull that together. It took *some*, and she's got it. It still knocks me right out. To me, it sounds better than most of her records of that time."

"I flipped out over it," Chips agrees of the record. "The only thing I found wrong and I still find wrong: Obviously,

Rick Hall's machine and the machine in New York were traveling at a slightly different speed. The piano is out of tune on that record, and it bothered me immensely. The piano is sharp to the track. If you listen to the piano, you hear it—it's almost a quarter-tone sharp to the track." He's right. "Do Right Woman" is one of Aretha's supreme achievements, a moving, deep, stripped-down, pleading yet forceful number, and a prime example of Franklin's ability to stray from a melody, embellish a phrase, and yet do so simply, without "oversouling," to use another Jerry Wexler coinage. But if you listen closely to the track, every few musical phrases one can indeed discern a slight key discrepancy. The error is not enough to damage the impact of the record, but it is apparent if you listen for it.

Despite the minor screw-up, "Do Right Woman" is a great Aretha Franklin record, and a terrific example of the intersection of country and soul that the Fame players had in their bones. "That was really a country song," Ted White says rightly. "But Aretha kind of flavored it up a bit, gave it a soulful feeling." "Do Right Woman" is all about timing and restraint: The woman known for impossible flights of improvisation does relatively little, riff-wise, on the tune, instead allowing the emotion to emerge from the natural tonal quality of her voice. "I like her voice quality better on this than on 'I Never Loved a Man,'" Wexler told me, almost surprising himself. "Much more presence.

There were no horns on this record. No strings, no wood-winds, no nothing." What there is, is a languor, a relaxed, unhurried ease to Aretha's singing, and that effect infuses the lyric with a kind of world-weariness that's palpable when she sings, "A woman's only human/This you should understand/She's not just a plaything/She's flesh and blood, just like a man," a phrase that gains in force as she repeats it later in the song. The first time it's a reminder to respect her as a woman; the second time it's a demand. And yet no matter how strong her tone as she addresses a man in this and other songs, she seems to do so in a loving way. She's not angry with her man; she's trying to be patient, thoughtful, wise. Aretha's own personal, real-life romantic relationships were fraught with difficulty, but when she sings about matters of the heart, she sounds as if she knows everything there is to know about humanity, love, and the complexities of both.

Aretha had been able to complete "Do Right Woman" essentially on her own, with just her sisters and Cissy helping her to take the rough tracks recorded in Muscle Shoals and turn them into a lasting bit of soul. To com-plete an album, she needed the assistance of her newly dis-covered (and very nearly lost) rhythm section. Franklin had been a professional New York City musician for years; the Southern boys, on the other hand, were new to the Big Apple, and being in the city, roughly a thousand miles and a world away from their corner of northwest Alabama, was both exhilarating and daunting.

Spooner had visited the city once before, as a teenager. "I went to New York City in 1961, on a high school class trip," he recalls in his endearingly languid mode of expression. "We rented a Greyhound bus, with the driver with the cap, and I think one of the teachers was a chaperone. It was a wonderful trip—I loved it to death."

This time, they flew: "We made our first jet flight, from Memphis—727 gonna take you to heaven," Jimmy Johnson says merrily. "We got out of that plane, and I've got my guitar in my hand, and I'm lookin' up. There was so much going on in one city block, I'd get a migraine headache on the way to the studio. I had to lie down for about an hour before I could play."

One can't help but imagine these immensely talented but unavoidably provincial Alabama boys, still only twenty-four years old, tops, schlepping their gear through the city streets, staring up at skyscrapers, dodging traffic, admiring the unprecedentedly posh (for them) Essex House Hotel, where they were put up. But though green from a major metropolis standpoint, once they got into the studio they were pros, and the Curtis sessions went quickly. Aretha joined them as these sessions wound down to lay tracks for "Save Me," a compositional collaboration among King Curtis, Aretha, and her sister Carolyn, who was developing into a strong songwriter in her own right.

"Save Me," "a dance number," as Wexler describes it, was the right kind of song to establish an upbeat, feel-good vibe in the studio. With its driving, almost circular bass line, Aretha's sassy, girlish vocal, and the powerfully punctuating horn blasts, the two-minute twenty-one-second song is wildly enjoyable, if something of a trifle. Nina Simone would record, a few years later, a less funky, angrier version, but for all the enthusiasm that's greeted the song over the years, "Save Me" is more an extended riff than a fully constructed song with mood-shifting chord changes and sections to steer a listener's emotions. But at that point, in the studio, no one cared: The track was funky, Aretha's singing sublime, and it set the right tone for the resurrection of Franklin's career as an Atlantic artist. With "Save Me" in the can, Aretha took a few days to work on some arrangements, and on February 14, 1967—Valentine's Day—the group reconvened to record what would become Aretha's most enduring piece of work.

Otis Redding's "Respect," all playful horns and sexy, mock-beleaguered vocals, was a top five R&B hit in 1965 and one of the highlights of the influential *Otis Blue* album. The lyric, in Otis's hands, is a fairly straightforward appeal from man to woman that she show him sufficient appreciation for bringing home the bacon, as it were. It's clear-cut, a song without subtext. Redding's version is characteristically funky, with his raspy-soulful singing and electric vocal charisma front and center. It's a wonderful track but not a record that would necessarily have the same kind of cultural impact as other Redding classics, such as "Mr. Pitiful," "Try a Little Tenderness," or "(Sittin' On) The Dock of the Bay" (though, to be sure, there are listeners who would argue with that assessment). As reported in Scott Freeman's biography of the singer, there are also lingering questions over the tune's authorship. Redding most likely got the song's conceptual basis from his good friend and road manager, songwriter Speedo Sims, who in turn may have gotten some material for the song from a group of which he was a part.

In a certain sense, it doesn't matter who originally wrote the song, because Aretha Franklin, ever since February 14, 1967, has owned "Respect." As DJ-turned-Congresswoman Louise Bishop has stated that Aretha had been performing "Respect" as part of her live show for a good year before she recorded her epoch-making version for *I Never Loved a Man the Way I Love You*. She'd had time to settle into the song, to develop her own version—radically, almost unrecognizably different from Redding's original. In their song-selecting preproduction meetings prior to the initial Muscle Shoals date, which would often take place at his house in Great Neck, Jerry and Aretha had gone over possibilities for inclusion on the album. Franklin suggested "Respect," and Wexler, the executive who oversaw Otis's career and a profound Redding admirer, was happy to comply. But, he told me, he had no idea that Aretha would turn the song inside out, would alter the feel, overhaul the melody, would so thoroughly and effectively impose her own musical vision onto it.

"She walked in with this," Wexler says, seemingly still in disbelief over the apparent ease with which the singer reinvented and improved on a song by the seriously talented Otis Redding. "I had no notion. I didn't know what she had in mind. Aretha was terrific at setting up a song the way she wanted it to go. Many of the songs she would bring in—basically the cake was in the oven; all you had to do was bake it. She would work out the rhythm part, the piano arrangement, she worked out her vocals, she'd bring in her backup singers. When they came in singing 'Respect,' they had the whole template. They had everything."

Turkish-born Arif Mardin, credited as an engineer on the session but in fact more of an associate producer, remembers it similarly. "I would be out there in the studio, pencil and music paper in hand, trying to ascertain what Aretha would be playing on the piano," he told me. "I would write down chord changes. The guitar player would look at her right hand and find out what position she was using; the bass player would listen to her left hand and try to come up with a bass line. This all stemmed from her piano. And then, like cooks, we would make the soup and everybody would add an ingredient. Very few people make records like that today. It was fantastic—the interplay was wonderful and people bounced off each other. And she would drill the backup singers to perfection."

Wexler, too, asserts that Aretha "arranged the records at home. The arrangements were the top line of the vocal, the chord sequence, the rhythm pattern, and the layout. She plays this, and the guys listen to a couple of passes, and they've got it. Because when she comes in it's all there." Wexler recalls that not all the great musicians he worked with were as quick to adapt to this process favored by the Southern players. "When I took Bob Dylan to Muscle Shoals, he had no way of knowing what the method was, and I wasn't about to say, Bob, you gotta do this, you gotta do that," Wex recalls. "So he started playing on every track and singing on every track. And it was a disaster. We only made one song. So we went back to the house—we rented a house, the musicians, Bob, and I—and we played back this song, and it was like mortuary time. Death. I bring Bob Dylan to Muscle Shoals and this is what I've done. So the next day I managed to figure it out: First of all, I said, Bob, don't be playing until I tell you to play. And instead of isolating everybody, I put them all together on the floor, and they fed off each other. Of course, we had leakage forever. But I had the engineer run a quarter-inch tape after they got into a groove. When they got to where it needed to be, I fed back what they had done and had them play along. So they were playing along to a groove they had already set. After a couple of passes we knew we had it. We made four songs that day and finished the record by Friday. Don't ask me how. I never spoke to anyone who used this device. It was improvisation, but somehow . . . and Bob was very happy."

David Ritz rightly credits Wexler with a similarly inventive savvy in insisting that Aretha take the lead on piano: "He encouraged her to play. She's kind of a reactive person. She reacted to Jerry saying, 'Sit down and play.' 'Well, I'm here, hmm, look at what I'm coming up with!' He definitely empowered her. She took the leap. I think she looked at Atlantic as the label of Ruth Brown and Ray Charles, and I think she saw Jerry as a very authoritative guy, very direct and assertive and proactive in the studio. And she was cool with that, because at that point in her career she was open to be led."

The background vocals both Mardin and Wexler refer to, sung by Erma and Carolyn Franklin, who flew East for the occasion, are a tour de force, from the instantly recognizable sock-it-to-mes, which undeniably constituted a sexual demand (despite Aretha's coy protestations to the contrary), to the repetition of "re-re-re," offered seven times until, on the eighth go-round, the entire word made its way out of the sisters' mouths: *respect*. "Re-re-re—that's what they called Aretha," Wexler notes. "It was a very ingenious variation, coming up with the 're' for 'respect,' because she's commonly called Ree by her sister girls." To take that idea and run with it wildly, Aretha, with the support of her sisters thus intoning her nickname, verily *becomes* the concept she's singing about. It's a kind of R&B quasi-syllogism: Aretha is respect is Aretha.

But this deconstruction of the song's title term is nevertheless not the most effective in the number. Fans can hear Franklin's "Respect" hundreds and hundreds of times, and every time she makes her mind-blowing entrance on the heels of the fourth verse, with just a few carefully spaced instrumental blasts behind her, and spells out, "R-E-S-P-E-C-T/Find out what it means to me/R-E-S-P-E-C-T/Take care of TCB," they get chills. In a 1979 essay, Sherley Anne Williams says of this soul spelling lesson, "Aretha characterized respect as something given with force and great effort and cost. And when she even went so far as to spell the word 'respect,' we just knew that this sister wasn't playing around about getting Respect and keeping it." Even the use of the slang term "TCB," meaning "take care of business" and commonly used in the black community at the time, adds to the force with which Franklin demands props. It's so important and inarguable a matter in the relationship she sings of in the song as to be practically a business transaction. The moment is almost absurdly powerful, and in 1967, when Aretha demanded, with such ferocity, that the world find out what respect meant to her, the effect was not just novel but startling and exhilarating.

Wexler states that the arrangement was all there when Aretha walked in the door. But he also recalls that, in fact, the song lacked a proper bridge (shades of "Do Right Woman"), as it did on Redding's original as well. "Respect," in Aretha's hands, is a song that *needs* a bridge—a momentary break midsong to let listeners relax, collect themselves, recognize and absorb the tension, and prepare for the imminent resumption of Aretha's assertive yet flirtatious singing. Redding (or Speedo Sims, or whoever) had composed no bridge, so the guys set their minds on the question of whence they could pilfer a suitable musical breakdown. Someone had the inspiration—Wexler thinks it was King Curtis—to turn to a Sam-and-Dave number. "Even with her additions and her editorial emendation of the song, it didn't have a bridge," Wexler explains. "So while we were doing it we thought, we'll put in a four-bar bridge. And we took the bridge from 'When Something Is

Wrong with My Baby' by Sam and Dave. It's great because it provides fantastic release. It feels like a key change."

Mardin recalls that, in fact, the group had just recorded "When Something Is Wrong with My Baby" a few days earlier for Curtis's "Memphis Hits" session, so the song was indeed fresh in everybody's mind. "We thought, How could we lift this song up?" Mardin says of the still-forming version of the Redding song. "'Respect' is in C. But that bridge, Curtis's saxophone solo is in F sharp—a totally un-related key, but we liked it! We liked those chords! So we put it in. And then, from the F sharp, 'Respect' starts with a G chord—the five of the G. So from the F sharp we went to the G—it *sounded* like a half-tone modulation, but it wasn't. It was a very interesting solo construction and we did it right there. There was nothing haphazard on Aretha's part. But the way we came up with that strange key change, which led back naturally—it was done there on the spot. She didn't mind—and she had to learn those chords, to play on the piano. She's open to suggestions. She has her musical ideas, she knows what she wants to do, but she's open."

"As a recording artist, she's very much a collaborator," Ritz picks up. "And that's the spirit of rhythm and blues. It's a collaborative art form, and I think she's very much in that tradition: Let's get together and jam, and see what we come up with. There's a guy named Bobby Scott, a great musician, who wrote 'He Ain't Heavy, He's My Brother.' And Bobby did these Marvin Gaye charts for an album called *Vulnerable,* which was released after Marvin was killed, and he did a bunch of those Columbia charts for Aretha. And he said he's never been in the studio with an artist who was more cooperative than Aretha. Marvin put him through some changes. But he said Aretha was a dream."

Recording "Respect" and the four other songs that were cut that day established a process this crew would utilize on all future sessions with the singer, whereby Aretha and the band would perform all the instrumental tracks, with Franklin providing a temporary scratch vocal, which would be discarded, to help the players follow a song's form. Once a satisfactory rhythm track had been laid down, Aretha, alone in the studio, would record her vocal part as the musicians, engineers and producer watched and listened from behind the vast pane of glass separating the studio floor from the control booth. "The second we got the track, she would get up from the piano and walk straight to the vocal mic," Jimmy Johnson explains of "Respect" and subsequent numbers. "We looked like a caterpillar: We walked one after the other straight into the control room, in the front row, and sat down—never, ever, *not* to be frozen to death by her performance. Chill bones."

Wexler, Dowd, Mardin (who would go on to produce later Aretha efforts), the band, et al. may have been dazzled by each vocal take, but Aretha herself generally thought she could do better. "We'd very often redo her vocals at her request," Wexler reminisces. "Because she could envision—she really is a genius—she could envision a better way to go. As a producer I would ask a singer sometimes, Give me another one, and I'd tell them what I wanted. I couldn't tell her what I wanted—I didn't know. But *she* knew. And she'd lay down a vocal, and I'd say, Hey, that's great—we're done. And she'd say, 'Oh, wait, I've got something else.' And she'd go some other place with it. I was aware I was the recipient of some genius work." ("You don't know what we discarded," Mardin says tantalizingly of the scratched vocal takes.)

When Aretha had achieved a vocal take on "Respect" that satisfied her, there was a general euphoria in the room. "You could tell instantly it was major," Ted White told me. "It was phenomenal." A few weeks later, when Wexler played the cut for Redding, the song's originator, he famously exclaimed, as Wexler remembers it for me, "Looks like that little gal done took my song." Feigning outrage, he instructed Jerry to burn the master. "He was very jovial about it," Wexler laughs.

Redding was one of three male titans of soul whose work Aretha would cover on this busy day of recording—though no woman artist was given a tip of the hat, an interesting omission. It's as if Aretha sought to align herself, straight out of the gate, with her legendary R&B forebears, and it's noteworthy that such role models were mainly men. Throughout her career, Aretha has covered countless songs by major male recording artists: Paul McCartney's "Let It Be," Paul Simon's "Bridge Over Troubled Water," Marvin Gaye's "Wholly Holy," the Rolling Stones' "Satisfaction," and on this day Ray Charles's "Drown in My Own Tears" and Sam Cooke's "A Change Is Gonna Come" and "Good Times." Her output of songs associated with other women singers, however, is relatively sparse (though there are, of course, prominent exceptions, such as the Dionne Warwick–associated "I Say a Little Prayer" and Dusty Springfield's "Son of a Preacher Man," among others). With the release of *I Never Loved a Man*, Aretha would instantly become an icon of black femaleness, and women would form an enormous sector of her fan base. "Aretha let her raggedy edges show, which meant she could be trusted with ours," writes Thulani Davis of Sister Ree and her female fans. But musically, it appears that Franklin felt only a secondary affinity for her fellow women artists (with exceptions), or at least failed to be deeply inspired by them. Perhaps it's a healthy (or not so healthy) sense of competition with other female singers; perhaps she felt more of a challenge retrofitting the work of her male counterparts to her own talents; perhaps she tactfully chose to demur from blowing her female colleagues out of the water with her own powerhouse versions of their songs (though this last is so unlikely as to be comical). Most likely, Aretha merely saw herself (rightly) as occupying the same artistic terrain as the major musical trailblazers she admired, a group mainly comprised of men. She adored Dinah Washington and had recorded a tribute album to that singer for Columbia Records, but for the most part, the artists who, at the time, were driving pop and soul music into new realms were men. Aretha, in some sense, had to master the output of these male musical figures to prove her own genius. It's an almost prefeminist case of having to do a man's job better than a man in order to garner the proper respect.

Tackling "Drown in My Own Tears," written by musical jack-of-all-trades Henry Glover and recorded indelibly by Ray Charles, and "A Change Is Gonna Come," the great Sam Cooke's signature song and "magnum opus" in author Peter Guralnick's words, required considerable courage, but Aretha wasn't lacking in confidence of her gifts. "Drown in My Own Tears," track two on *I Never Loved a Man,* is a blues song, soulful and mournful in Brother Ray's version. Not the way Aretha sings it. "This isn't blues. This is gospel," says Jerry as we listen to the song together. "The whole record builds beautifully in intensity. It gets better as it goes along. Beautiful rendition."

"Drown in My Own Tears" doesn't get a lot of attention in discussions of *I Never Loved a Man*, which generally center on "Respect," the title track, and perhaps "Dr. Feelgood." But it's an important addition to the album's track listing precisely for the merger of blues and gospel in Aretha's version. The song, in fact, is such a perfect melding of the two genres that all evidence of its blues structure and feel and gospel vocalism virtually falls by the wayside to make room for something new, something distinctly "Aretha." One can feel the blues and feel the gospel in the song, but more than that one feels Aretha's emerging and unique musical identity, that now legendary ability to put her own stamp on any song she essays, to funnel disparate musical vernaculars through her system to create something new, unpredictable, and striking. Wexler makes an interesting point regarding this song's background vocals (which were always an important element in Aretha's Atlantic sides), noting that the backup is much more effective when the girls sing full phrases rather than mere individual syllables. Aretha sings a phrase, and Carolyn, Erma, and Cissy respond, singing "you" in three-part harmony. "I don't like 'you,'" Wexler grimaces (and for a moment I'm offended). "One syllable is not cogent—it sounds like a horn chart." Before he can finish, the girls enter again, this time singing, "You come on home," and stretching the final word to five syllables. "*This* I like!" he exclaims, before launching into a list of things he'd do differently with the recording now, years later: "I'd take the echo off her voice, I'd have more projection. I would remove some of those chops in the vocal responses. It's a little too bottomy. It's not her fault. It ain't her. It's the way the mic was picking her up. But she's sure doing a beautiful vocal." (He concedes, however, that "I like Ray Charles's better. . . .") Wexler's stellar R&B sensibility is intact, and kicks in the moment we press play. But it's somehow surprising to hear the producer of this great album enumerating ways in which a particular song might be improved.

Otis and Ray were artists Aretha admired; Sam Cooke was her idol. It must have been daunting for her to tackle "A Change Is Gonna Come," not just one of Cooke's greatest songs, but a penetrating social statement of racial pride and resilience. The song was inspired by the recent success of Bob Dylan's "Blowin' in the Wind," and was intended as Cooke's proud and heartfelt entry in the domain of socially conscious, perspective–altering music. Sam's song is a masterpiece, deeply felt and, more important, gorgeously sung. ("Sam—magic," says Wexler, shaking his head in disbelief at the singer's talent.) If there's a charge to be leveled at Sam Cooke's "A Change Is Gonna Come," it's that the recording is a bit bombastic, with its vibrato-heavy strings and somber, muted horn arrangements. Of course, these are minor quibbles with a superb record, elevated to genius level by Sam's sweet, sexy, immediate, familiar yet otherworldly vocals. As gospel-trained pop singers go, perhaps only Sam Cooke could give Aretha Franklin a run for her money.

Aretha goes in a different direction with the song, turning Cooke's widereaching social commentary into a sparer, more personal statement. In Aretha's version, "A Change Is Gonna Come" morphs from Sam's position on the world into Aretha's tribute to Sam, who had been killed in a sordid hotel mishap less than three years before. Cooke launches straight into the verse in his rendition; Aretha composes a personal paean to Sam, a kind of R&B recitative to set up the remainder of the song. "There's an old friend that/I once heard say/something that touched my heart/And it began this way," she sings with emotion, backing herself on solo piano. It's ironic that Aretha, much more involved in supporting the Civil Rights Movement than was Cooke, thanks to her association with King, would take Sam's song and, in effect, tone down its civil rights implications. She would leave that subtext intact, but performing a kind of meta "Change Is Gonna Come," directing attention from the outset to the song's creator more than to the original intentions of its lyrical content. Wexler notes astutely, moreover, that in several places Franklin adjusts the lyric from "a change is gonna come" to "*my* change is gonna come." "I always thought it was odd that she says, 'my change,'" Wexler told me. "When a woman talks about her change, she's talking about menopause." It's an interesting and undeniable quirk of her interpretation, one that once again draws attention to the singer's womanness; but in fact Aretha sings the song as a kind of narrator, putting the words of the song in her mentor's mouth rather than her own, encircling Cooke's phrases with "he said." In effect, the song is Aretha's artistic opportunity to *become* Sam Cooke, which in a sense had been her crossover goal all along.

The other two songs that day were less intense lyrically, and the recorded results were not quite as overpowering as the Charles and Cooke numbers. But they were nonetheless vital, ultimately, to the identity of the album and to Aretha's artistic development, because they were her own compositions. Aretha recorded four originals during six years at Columbia; by the end of this second day at Atlantic's studios, she'd complete her third self-penned tune for her new label. "Don't Let Me Lose This Dream," written with Ted, and "Baby, Baby, Baby," coauthored by sister Carolyn, are somewhat incongruous with the rest of the album (and even with the other Aretha originals recorded on other days for the project, "Save Me" and "Dr. Feelgood"). These two numbers represent her striving for a kind of slick-pop respectability, which suggests she wasn't made all that miserable by similar stylistic forays at Columbia. "It's much more pop than the other songs," Wexler says of "Don't Let Me Lose This Dream." "It's almost Motownish, instead of Atlanticish." Jerry doesn't love this pair of songs but says, "In spite of my tepid feeling, it's very important— it's another side of Aretha that engages a hell of a lot of her audience. The cadence, the way the words flow together, the rhythm—it's her thinking. It's a love song."

"Don't Let Me Lose This Dream" has an appealing Latin feel and great singing, though its lyrics ("Help me hold on to this dream/'Cause sometime dreams often come true/And they'll come true, they'll come true/For me and you") are fairly earnest, even hokey. "Baby, Baby, Baby," though a straight-ahead ballad, is more interesting be-cause it challenges the widely held notion that Aretha unfailingly sings from a position of strength or author-ity. "She would never do a song of self-pity," Wexler says. "The scorned woman, the hurt woman—come back please, one more chance. That was absolutely out." It's easy to understand why Wexler would make such a com-ment; Aretha's singing is so unprecedentedly gripping, no matter what she sings, that she habitually comes across as in control, if not wholly invulnerable. But there are plenty of instances, lyrically speaking, where Aretha *is* the scorned woman, the hurt woman. On "Baby, Baby,

Baby," for example, she sings "I didn't mean to hurt you/Don't you know that I'd rather hurt myself," and those are words she herself wrote. Even "I Never Loved a Man" is sung from a position of subjugation (writer Brian Ward accurately says the song has "masochistic undertones"), as Aretha admits, almost powerlessly, to having been inescapably snared by a no-good liar and cheat. What's remarkable is that in many of her songs, including these original compositions, Aretha casts herself in a kind of weak, blindly-devoted-to-her-man role, and yet she never *sounds* like a victim. "Men get to her," one close observer of Aretha told me. "She wants to please them." It's certainly evident that she sought to please her father, and in the late 1960s, there was some confusion as she tried to simultaneously please both Wexler and White, the most important men in her life at the time. What makes Aretha's music so compelling to female listeners is that she assumes the perennial role of woman who aims to please her man—and turns that struggle into art, paying tribute to an old-fashioned gender system in which women are caregivers. She embraces this ordinary position, and with her extraordinary vocalism makes it honorable. Aretha loves men and has always viewed housewifehood as a desirable, rewarding way of life. She sees herself as a domestic creature and, musically, finds power in that position. As a result, the Aretha Franklin who emerges on *I Never Loved a Man* is an extremely modern,

progressive kind of feminist, one who doesn't reject traditional womanly roles but sees the gratification that can be
derived from them and celebrates those conventional yet
satisfying possibilities.

On *I Never Loved a Man*, Aretha knows what she needs
as a woman, and one of those things is sex. That was the
focus of the original tune that would be recorded in New
York the following day: "Dr. Feelgood." Subtitled mock-
portentously "Love Is a Serious Business," the song is a
major piece of music-making and singing, one of the most
enduring songs in Franklin's catalogue. In a certain regard,
"Dr. Feelgood" is the quintessential Aretha Franklin song,
as it brings together almost every theme for which her
music and professional persona are known: the big-chord
gospel pianism; the underlying blues framework of the
song; the insistent yet elegant demand for sexual satisfaction; the feminist underpinnings of so brazenly making
such a demand; and, above all, the soaring, proud vocal
performance.

"She was quiet." "She deferred a lot to Jerry and her
husband." "There was never any communication with her
except through Ted." This is how those who were present
describe Aretha's demeanor at the *I Never Loved a Man*
sessions. And yet this apparently shy woman was capable
of opening her mouth and belting out, "I don't want nobody always sitting around me and my man. . . . Now, I

don't mind company, because company's all right with me every once in a while. But, oh, when me and that man get to lovin', I tell you girls, I dig you, but I just don't have time to sit and chit and sit and chit-chat and smile. . . . Got me a man named Dr. Feelgood, and oh, yeah, that man takes care of all my pains and my ills. . . . And taking care of business is really this man's game." These were words she wrote. Wexler calls "Respect" a demand for "sexual attention of the highest order"; "Dr. Feelgood" is perhaps an even stronger declaration (and celebration) of sexual need. This was the preacher's daughter talking about—insisting on—sex and doing so with true gospel fervor. "It's one of her most impassioned vocals by far," Wexler told me rightly. "Good God almighty, the man sure makes me feel real good," Aretha concludes the song over a sustained and rumbling piano chord straight out of the church. It's the kind of out-of-time, worshipful moment typical of gospel music, where as a song seemingly approaches its conclusion, the singer halts the action and spins the song into a new direction, expressing whatever musical or religious spirit has seized him or her. On live versions of "Dr. Feelgood" (most notably the classic, extended rendition of the *Live at Fillmore West* album), Aretha does just that, turning the song's denouement into a church service. The song, recorded on the third and final day of the *I Never Loved a Man* sessions, exemplifies the knotty but rich confluence of spirituality, sex, and the blues that characterized Aretha's upbringing and her subsequent musical identity.

A lyrics-added rendition of King Curtis's "Soul Serenade" and a jaunty take on Sam Cooke's more wistful "Good Times" ("filler," Jerry Wexler calls it) were also laid down that day, and with that, *I Never Loved a Man the Way I Love You*, Aretha Franklin's Atlantic Records debut, "one of the most remarkable reinventions in pop music," was in the can. Aretha was off to the races.

So were the Muscle Shoals players. If their Wilson Pickett work had endeared them to Wexler, their contributions to *I Never Loved a Man* made them suddenly indispensable to the Atlantic operation in the executive's mind. The boys would become fixtures on the label's output well into the next decade, and when Jimmy, Roger, and David severed ties to Rick Hall and established Muscle Shoals Sound Studios in Sheffield, Alabama, Wexler helped back the venture.

"He became the rhythm section's second daddy," Johnson recalls fondly, almost reverentially. "He took us under his wing. He was flying us to New York—me, Spooner, Roger, Tommy. And on Sundays, he would have his limo driver pick us up and drive us up to his home in Great Neck. We'd have meals, total family communication with everybody, Shirley and the kids. And we'd all sit around the pool, and Pickett would come over and Jerry and him would swim. It was great. He taught the rednecks how to drink Chateau Lafitte Rothschild! And we didn't like it! 'Cause it wadn't sweet. But after about two years of that we was guzzling. He really took care of us."

The guys almost without exception see this first bit of work with Aretha as the consummation of their musical marriage to Wexler and Atlantic, and each has fond and vivid memories of the sessions at Muscle Shoals and New York. "It sits right at the top of my satisfaction scale of things I've done," Spooner Oldham told me. "Most of those songs have held up. I don't feel cheated when I hear that stuff. Time has not made it weird." Dan Penn concurs: "I have seen, in my day, many important sessions—course I missed a lot of them too! But I been in some that really made my hair stand up, and that was right up there with the best of them. Aretha's session was spectacular."

To his regret, Chips Moman missed most of the resurrected session work in New York, playing guitar on King Curtis's "Save Me" before having to split, returning to Memphis for a previously scheduled project at his American Studios. Three years later, Aretha would record another Penn-Moman collaboration, "Dark End of the Street," but Chips would never work directly with Franklin again. "Baby here I be's, by the railroad track," he sang to me, echoing the song from Aretha's professional recorded debut. The song he'd written with Penn, "Do Right Woman—Do Right Man," had been completed in his absence, would become a soul-music classic in Aretha's hands. But Chips hadn't been there to see it. White, Laxton, the blow-up—the derailment of that first day of recording would force Chips out of the loop. But he wouldn't forget that first day, or Aretha's artistry. At the close of our rollicking, enjoyable conversation, during which we spoke about Moman's work with Elvis Presley, Willie Nelson, and other luminaries, Chips asked me poignantly, "Do you ever talk to Aretha? I would just like to let her know that I'm trying to say hello after all these years. I never could even tell her thank-you for such a wonderful job on my song."

nine

"It's 'Retha"

*I*t was as if the millennium had arrived." That's how Peter Guralnick describes the release of the single "I Never Loved a Man (the Way I Love You)," recalling the scene outside his local Boston record store the day the record hit stores. "People were dancing on the frosty street with themselves or with one another and lining up at the counter to get a purchase on that magic sound as the record kept playing over and over." It's a futuristic yet spiritual, quasi-religious image, this notion of a new, uncharted musical and cultural plane being summoned by Aretha, and one that's particularly apt, as Aretha—on all the songs on the album—turned to her church roots, filtered those influences through her own unique artistic sensibility, and produced something utterly new and forward-looking. "I Never Loved a Man," with "Do Right

Woman" as its B-side, was released on February 10, 1967 (days before the bulk of the rest of the album was even recorded), and on March 25 (Aretha's twenty-fifth birthday) reached number one on the R&B charts. The song would peak at number nine on the pop list. Two months later, "Respect" would hit the airwaves and subsequently conquer both the R&B and pop charts. Both songs quickly sold a million copies each.

"It was the greatest rhythm and blues music ever made," Ahmet Ertegun told me of *I Never Loved a Man*, when asked about the popular response to the album's first two singles. "That was it. I mean, you went to Copenhagen and you went dancing in a club and you danced to 'Respect.' You went to Singapore the next day and you danced to 'Respect.' You went to Johannesburg and you would dance to 'Respect.' And then you went to Buffalo, New York, and you danced to 'Respect.' That was it!"

"The reaction was fantastic," Wexler agrees. "It's a fantastic feminist statement. And it was in an instant every place."

Ted White recalls near shock the first time he heard "I Never Loved a Man" outside the studio. "Having been involved with the birth of that song, it was like being a parent. That first time I heard it on the radio, it just paralyzed me."

He wasn't the only one. "People went bananas," Louise Bishop remembers. "Absolutely bananas. 'I Never Loved a Man' was the most played song at that time. I can't even remember what else was out! It became the national anthem on all of the rock stations across the country. The tone, the music, the production—it had everything. Aretha can sing any other singer under the table, off the stage. When she wants to. There's no one that even comes close to her—when she wants to sing. So I just think that it was what people were waiting for. And they got it. And they got it again and again."

Black-music journalist (and, today, Columbia School of Journalism professor) Phyl Garland famously called "Respect" the "new black national anthem," in her book *The Sound of Soul*, released two years after the record. "We were waiting for that song," Garland told me of "Respect." "It exploded, and it was something we all fell in love with. She spoke to everyone. The *way* she interpreted it—we couldn't hear it enough." Garland echoes black feminist scholar Patricia Hill Collins, who wrote, "Even though the lyrics [to 'Respect'] can be sung by anyone, they take on special meaning when sung by Aretha in the way that she sings them." It's notable that while both these astute listeners recognize that there was something different and significant in Aretha's performance of the song, neither can quite pin down how: "the way she sings" must suffice. This semantic lapse is near universal when describing Aretha's singing; how can one properly put into words something so mystical, so spiritual, as Aretha Franklin's voice, especially when married to material that resonated so wholly with such a vast audience?

"Respect" came out, "and it was like, Oh my God, Aretha's covering Otis," Nikki Giovanni recalls. "I could not get to the record store fast enough to get that album. I had just graduated from college. And everybody started to say, Did you hear what she *did?* Everybody started to analyze that album. The Civil Rights Movement was *burning.* And I was aware that this was going to be *it.* And it actually is. I think the music has shown that Aretha capped an era."

The *New York Times* stated that " 'I Never Loved a Man the Way I Love You,' 'Do Right Woman' and 'Respect' shook the foundation of a complacent pop establishment and put Miss Franklin's star in orbit. Seated at the piano, surrounded by the band, her voice filled with mysterious sorrow, Franklin effectively reshaped popular music." The musicians on the album perceived the shift as well. "I thought it was the greatest thing I'd ever heard," David Hood says today of "I Never Loved a Man." "I thought that, all of a sudden, music had jumped up another level. It was such a great rhythm section—so young and exuberant and enthusiastic. It was just an incredible bringing together of talents, and it made a *new* thing. I'd always measured stuff against Sam and Dave or Otis Redding. This was above it. It was different. It had soul, but it was still accessible to white people. It had the best elements of pure black music and white music. That made it accessible. It really advanced the music from where it had been prior to that to a new level."

Dan Penn also emphasizes the musical commingling of black and white as essential to Aretha's—and indeed *all*—soul music. "To me, rhythm and blues is black singers with white record producers and songwriters," Penn said. "It is the mixture of the two colors of people in the studio. That's my rhythm and blues. That mixture produced a certain kind of music that people loved. I know I did." Wexler agrees, providing the unnecessary reminder that the Muscle Shoals musicians "were all Caucasians. This seems to confound perceived wisdom and logic of the music professors and commentators. How could authentic soul music and blues come out of a situation like this?"

The interracial arrangement was indeed a common practice; what elevated this particular recording into the apotheosis of soul was Franklin herself. "She was the artist," Dave Hood says. "Her stamp was all over it." It's worth addressing, in fact, just how indelible the Aretha imprint was on *I Never Loved a Man*. "Putting me back on piano helped Aretha-ize the new music," Franklin wrote. "This new Aretha music was raw and real and so much more myself. I loved it!"

"Aretha-ize" is the word for it. "I think this is really the beginning of Aretha as a coproducer," David Ritz, collaborator on Franklin's autobiography, told me. "The template for however many albums she did with Atlantic is there: She goes in, she sits down at the piano, the charts come together because *she's* the engine driving the locomotive. She's got it in her head—she's got the groove, she's got the harmonies. She's really a coproducer, and I think it was an inequity of the times that it just wasn't done that way. I think Jerry's great intelligence as a producer was that he kicked back and let her coproduce with him. And in a year or two, Isaac Hayes is doing *Hot Buttered Soul*, there's Curtis Mayfield, and then Marvin Gaye does *What's Going On?* They heard her dominance. It's not just, Get in there and sing the song. It's, I have an aural vision, and that vision will prevail."

It didn't hurt that Aretha's aural vision had the benefit of Atlantic's prodigious promotional efforts behind it. "After you work with Jerry Wexler and you see what a driving planner he is, you know you're dealing with success," sax player Charlie Chalmers told me. "We knew we were on a train that was going to run for a while." "It was the first

time we saw a record company in motion," drummer
Roger Hawkins recalls, marveling at the label's ability to
get a record heard and to move units. Aretha herself says
that "company promotion had something to do with the
records being successful," referring to the rapid-succession
follow-ups to *I Never Loved a Man: Aretha Arrives* (featur-
ing "Baby, I Love You"), *Lady Soul* ("A Natural Woman," in
fact, recorded the day after the *I Never Loved a Man* sides
were completed, but held for release, presumably because
its violin-laden arrangement didn't mesh with the rest of the
album), and *Aretha Now* ("Think"). All of which would sell
fabulously and help secure Franklin's reputation as the
Queen and make her a supremely in-demand performer
both at home and abroad. The marketing end of the record
industry in 1967 was a far cry from what it is today, when
label executives essentially decide which album will be a
hit and then make it so. But there was a developing star-
making machinery, and, to Aretha's benefit, Atlantic Records was one of its earliest and most effective adherents.

But in the end it was Aretha who pushed *I Never Loved
a Man* over the top thanks to the aural vision Ritz describes, and such a commitment to unfurling one's own
artistic self, undiluted, was at the time especially remarkable coming from a woman. By thus announcing herself as a
self-created female musical force to be reckoned with,
Aretha forever aligned herself with the two great jazz and

blues predecessors to whom John Hammond had years before compared her: Bessie Smith and Billie Holiday. This notion of continuity, of a kind of torch-passing among the major female figures in twentieth-century music is almost eerie. Hammond had scarcely finished overseeing Bessie's last recordings when he produced Billie's first. Billie had died just two years before, shortly after the release of her lushly produced but harrowingly sung *Lady in Satin* LP, when Hammond brought Aretha before the public. With *I Never Loved a Man*, Aretha firmly planted herself along the continuum of blues women started by Gertrude "Ma" Rainey and Smith and picked up by Holiday. If anything, Aretha has gotten woefully short shrift in terms of her musical contributions as they compare to those of her forebears, probably because, first, she hasn't died young or ignominiously; second, unlike Bessie and Billie, her status as an upstanding middle class citizen, for the most part, has never been called into question; and third, her hit-making ability has lent her an aura of "pop," a designation that doesn't often bring about the kind of canonical enshrinement that Bessie and Billie enjoy as blues and jazz artists.

In her terrific scholarly work *Blues Legacies and Black Feminism*, Angela Davis writes of the bawdy Bessie and "Ma" Rainey, "These blues women had no qualms about announcing female desire." One listen to Aretha's Atlantic debut, and the world knew that she didn't either. Diana Ross and the Supremes sang of their "baby love"; Aretha countered, in the parenthetical subtitle of "Dr. Feelgood," that "love is a serious business," and without good sex of the kind that Dr. Feelgood administers—"that man takes care of all of my pains and my ills"—there won't be a love that lasts. In the pre-*Ms.* late sixties, Aretha's assurance to her female listeners that they *needed* to get their grooves on was enormously influential. Bessie Smith may have similarly sought a man who could take care of business as early as the 1920s, but the chaste fifties put down something of a clamp on the acceptability of female sexual needs. "Dr. Feelgood" served as a rebuke to that outdated, Eisenhower-era notion and predicted the female sexual freedom musically celebrated in the disco era.

Indeed, because of the sheer power of her singing, not to mention her irreproachable demand for respect, the Aretha of *I Never Loved a Man* quickly grew to be viewed as the quintessential proverbial "strong woman." But in the mid-to-late 1960s, the strong black woman, at least within her own community, was becoming a virtual pariah. Nowadays, not a single female R&B or hip-hop artist would fail to characterize herself as strong—and many of them genuinely merit the designation (Missy Elliot

comes to mind). But as black nationalism came to promi-
nence in the midsixties, when *I Never Loved a Man* arrived
in record stores, the idea that a black matriarchal force
was a liability was gaining currency in the black community. As Davis writes, "Male dominance was considered a
necessary prerequisite for black liberation." The civil
protest in a song like "Respect," especially as sung by
Aretha, helped portray a rising call to anger among blacks
that should perhaps have been embraced by the powerful-
black-brother ethos of black nationalism. The relative
subjugation of women embraced by the Black Power
Movement scarcely had a chance in the face of Aretha's
artistry. "Respect" was a powerful demand for equal con-
sideration precisely because it was made by such an artisti-
cally authoritative woman.

Bonnie Raitt has said of Aretha, "I learned way more
about being a woman from listening to her sing 'Respect'
than I ever did from any man." What is it about Aretha that
makes people think of her as the embodiment of womanhood? I think it stems from the duality of her shy yet
strong personality and the sheer elemental quality of her
voice. She embodies two almost paradoxical extremes of
femaleness: the shy girlish woman who lives to please
her man, and the powerful, strong-willed woman who demands R-E-S-P-E-C-T. These are extremes that virtually
all women identify with at various points (what woman

hasn't variously thought of herself as ultrafeminine, designed to delight her partner, and yet a proud, complex, self-reliant, calls-it-as-she-sees-it person?). Aretha's claim on these complementary yet divergent notions has added authority because of the almost mystical power of her voice. Aretha's singing emanates from her diaphragm—it may as well emerge from her loins—and resounds with glory and with mystery, a sense of the unknowable. In that sense she is a kind of earth mother figure.

Angela Davis's analysis of Aretha's cultural position as a woman in relation to the growing black power movement is apropos, as Franklin's "Respect"—mainstream hit though it was—signaled a pop-cultural pivot from the implicit musical protests that characterized the height of the era of the Civil Rights Movement to a more explicit form of protest that was more in tune with black power. After "Respect" in 1967, the way was cleared for James Brown to release "Say It Loud (I'm Black and I'm Proud)" in 1968. Because of Aretha's family connection to Martin Luther King Jr., plus the extraordinary amount of relatively unheralded work she did on his behalf (she performed at countless Southern Christian Leadership Conference fundraising events throughout the sixties), she has always (rightly) been aligned with the Civil Rights Movement. But the authority and dangerousness with which she insisted on respect in a sense makes that song a kind of harbinger of the movement's demise in the face of still stronger forms of racial pride and antiwhite-establishment protest.

Of course, Jerry Wexler, for one, even today does not acknowledge the civil-rights implications of "Respect." "There was no racial component to this," he told me, surprisingly. "It was universally feminist. She is a tremendous promulgator of her race—the things she did for Martin Luther King." But "Respect" was nevertheless solely "a great feminist statement combined with a sexual leavening." One assumes that Wexler prefers to avoid a knotty racial dialogue, because there's no denying—or missing—the novelty of a black woman requiring that she be treated with respect of all varieties, in 1967. ("Jerry Wexler wasn't living through the experience," Phyl Garland says mordantly.) Nikki Giovanni adores Wexler: "There is nothing about Jerry Wexler that is not to love, and I'm sure there are many people who would disagree with me, but I don't want to hear it." Nevertheless, when it comes to Wex's dismissal of "Respect" as a song of extreme importance to blacks, Giovanni, like Garland, is having none of it. "I'm not going to let Jerry get away with that," she says. " 'Respect' is so black. Hell, I was traveling in Africa in seventy-two, and that's a song that everybody knew. That and '(Say It Loud) I'm Black and I'm Proud.' And people who didn't speak English could say to me 'James Brown,' and I could raise my fist and say 'Say it loud,' and they'd say, 'I'm black and I'm proud.' It was a connection. And 'R-E-S-P-E-C-T' was the same thing. I'm visiting schools and *all* the kids know that. That song was about the dispossessed."

That is what made Aretha's arrival so extraordinary, unprecedented, and influential: She wasn't just a woman demanding respect at a moment when feminism was still hitting its stride; she wasn't a black man insisting on equal rights. She was a black woman, one who appealed to both men and women, blacks and whites, who asserted herself, who literally gave voice to her spiritual and sexual needs in a manner that made it impossible to begrudge her anything. The effect on a mainstream audience in 1967 was downright shocking.

And galvanizing. Music critic Nelson George says of the cultural moment following the release of *I Never Loved a Man*, "Aretha Franklin was not just indisputably the best singer in the R&B-soul world but the focus for, to use a sixties cliché, the positive spiritual energy of her listeners." What's more, "Despite singing love songs, many of them quite melancholy," George continues, "Franklin's voice communicated so wide a range of emotion as to truly defy description."

It's absolutely true that the singer resists analysis, and that's because for Aretha, music—life—is feeling. Her

singing is emotional, shifting, quicksilver, utterly unpredictable and mysterious. Was "sock it to me" meant to
have sexual connotations? When she says no, she may
sound coy, but she's being genuine, because for her the
line merely felt right, so she went with it. The music and
the emotion behind it *is* the message. She plans where her
music is headed and then allows it to make improvisational
detours along the way—but she doesn't plan a political or
social message, per se. Who cares what "sock it to me"
means? How does it make you *feel?* Aretha's music, in its
new, groundbreaking Atlantic Records incarnation, is elemental, metaphysical. And to some degree, analyzing it
detracts from its fundamentalness, from its "realness" and
hers.

Representative Bishop recalls a conversation she once
had with Aretha around the time of *I Never Loved a Man*
that illustrates the singer's hard-to-pin-down sense of self.
"I remember saying something to her once about how
record companies groomed their artists," Bishop remembers. "And she said to me, 'When I walk a certain way, it's
'Retha. When I sit a certain way, it' 'Retha. When I wear a
certain outfit, it's 'Retha. And I'm going to do what Aretha
wants to do.' And I never forgot that. That's the way
Aretha is. Maybe some people call her shy, maybe some
people say she has strange ways. But when you can sing,
and you are as gifted as Aretha is, you can be you! And she

brought me into line on that. She's Aretha! She's happy with herself. I don't think Aretha has ever had a day where she would have wanted to have been anyone else."

"She's one-hundred-percent artist," Giovanni agrees. "No one would ever do this, but if you had to compare her to any artist on earth, it would be Marilyn Monroe, but not nearly as tragic. Because Marilyn always knew who she was. And there were times when you saw her and she was Marilyn, and there were times when you saw her and she wasn't. And it was always interesting when she would turn the Marilyn on. Because she could be in a room and just be herself and nobody would even know, and then she'd do something, flick her hair. And Aretha's like that: mega, mega, mega watts. She doesn't always turn the light on. And sometimes she does. It's always Aretha. You have to be willing to say, 'Fuck you.' And very few people are. But Aretha always has been, and, as far as I've been able to see, remains at a fuck-you level. I don't think she's ever tried to make a hit. She's just going to sing *her* song. And who wouldn't?"

That strong sense of self, her firm, closely held knowledge, instilled in her by her father, that she was a Franklin and thus important (remember: unlike the trajectories of her fellow Detroiters-made-good, Aretha's is not a rags-to-riches story) makes Aretha Franklin somewhat impenetrable to all but her closest friends. "The great thing about her is that she tells the truth," says Ahmet Ertegun. "She tells it like it is. And if you don't like it, too bad. She's a wonderful person." And you feel that he means it. But unlike other artists whose personal lives are easy to read, Aretha is hard to get to know. Except when she sings. "I think the great irony," says David Ritz, "is that there's no tougher interview, in terms of holding stuff back. And in terms of artistry, there's no more forthcoming artist. The more closed down she is, the more opened up she is when she opens her mouth to sing. Because Lord, have mercy. Her voice isn't what it used to be, but she *still* fucks you up."

"In the history of Atlantic," Ahmet Ertegun told me, "our two shining stars are Ray Charles and Aretha Franklin. God knows we've had some great male singers—Otis Redding, Joe Turner. But there was no one better than Ray. And I think Aretha has a similar place among lady singers. Nobody questions the fact that she is *the* great singer of our time. She is the greatest soul singer of our time, and probably the greatest all-around singer of our time."

Because the material, the arrangements, the vibe allowed Franklin to "Aretha-ize" her music, the result was vastly more forthcoming than her previous work, and because of Aretha's astounding vocal gift, that artistry made soul music as a genre even more popular than it had been in the previous months when the Supremes and other such white-bread "soul" acts were dominating the R&B charts. With Aretha playing piano and singing gospel-influenced tunes with the bel canto–appreciating Atlantic Records behind her, everything came together. Aretha became the voice of a certain cultural sector, in the way that the Beatles or Elvis Presley had before and Marvin Gaye or even Michael Jackson would after. "Every historical period requires artistic explanation that's more emotional than intellectual," Ritz continues. "She's the emotional expression of the era, and the era was yearning for assertiveness of ethnic strength and pride. What was required to express these societal yearnings and confusions and aspirations was a voice of tremendous authority and penetrative fervor."

What was needed was a voice with soul, and Aretha, having that quality in abundance, instantly became the genre's queen. But in so doing, in taking the church-fueled blues of Ray Charles and turning it into the next big thing, accessible to all—even beloved by all—Franklin, in a certain sense, closed the door on the soul movement. Once Aretha "blew all asunder with 'I Never Loved a Man,'" as Gerri Hirshey put it, where else could soul possibly go?

Giovanni felt Franklin's fervor and wondered, in "Poem for Aretha," how the woman could possibly live up to the expectations heaped on her:

Nobody mentions how it feels to become a freak
Because you have talent and how
No one gives a damn how you feel
But only cares that Aretha Franklin is here like maybe
That'll stop:
> *Chickens from frying*
> *Eggs from being laid*
> *Crackers from hating*

"My poem said, Aretha was the voice, if she said come, it would have been done," Giovanni says today. "But you have to remember the worst was yet to come. Everybody knew the other foot would drop. Because by the time we get to 1968, we're in revolution. And I think that people are beginning to relook at 1968, because it was a murderous, vicious time, and yet we were willows, we bent but we didn't break. I would never ask Aretha, 'What do you think?' because she's a singer—she was supposed to say, 'This is where my heart is.' And what she did was put it out there. And in times of pain, we kept referencing that."

"Soul was the new imprint, was the new rubric. But I had a hunch," Jerry Wexler told an interviewer of this era with the benefit of hindsight. "I told my partner, I have a feeling this is going to grind to a sudden halt. I felt new things happening. One thing you could call the rising aspirations of the inner city—they were looking for other things than this so-called religious-based music. There was a new spirit. It was more secular. But of course, the thing that really seemed to cap it was the assassination of Dr. King."

ten

Ecstatic

*B*y many accounts, the services held April 9, 1968 for the Reverend Martin Luther King Jr. were something of a logistical shambles. The country had not yet mastered the art of staging epic public funerals. President Kennedy's service, possessed of no shortage of pomp and gravitas, was still fresh in the collective memory, but much of that day's outpouring of grief was carefully contained and strictly superintended inside St. Matthew's Cathedral and within the walls of Arlington National Cemetery. The final farewell to Martin, on the other hand, was held in Ebenezer Baptist Church, King's own ministry and a public venue smack in the middle of Atlanta. Dr. King had never shied away from the public, even on occasions when questions of safety would suggest that he ought to, and on this day the public would not shy away from him. Thousands flocked to 407 Auburn Avenue, blocking intersections, giving police fits, and falling over one another to pay final tribute to the slain leader. Organizers scarcely knew what had hit them and quickly found that controlling the throng and sticking to the script were going to be virtually impossible.

The streets outside the church were overcome by a kind of hushed frenzy, as devastated mourners pressed forward, desperate to get in, or at least get closer, but observing a near silence brought on by the solemnity of the occasion. Now and then a ripple of excitement coursed through the engorged horde with the arrival of a prominent statesman or celebrity. As limousines inched toward the building through the crush of onlookers, it was virtual bedlam: police officers screaming, "Move it back!"; a youthful Teddy Kennedy struggling to make his way a few yards from his car to the church threshold; the big-three network news correspondents confusedly trying to make some sense of and impose some order on the chaos of the day. The mania reached fever pitch with the arrival of a Goyaesque Jackie Kennedy, in a Spanish-looking black lace veil, her demeanor and dress instantly evoking that other national tragedy from less than five years before.

Inside Ebenezer, organ tones sounded as mourners made their way down the red-carpeted aisle toward King's casket, positioned front and center with white flowers in the shape of a cross placed on its cover. Eartha Kitt, Sammy Davis Jr., New York mayor John Lindsay, Nelson Rockefeller, Paul Newman, Leontyne Price, Sidney Poitier and a host of other prominent figures squeezed themselves into wooden pews that would shortly be filled to capacity. Harry Belafonte, perhaps Martin's closest confidant, was in tears before the service even began. They all waited patiently for Coretta Scott King, who, with her four children in tow (Yolanda, twelve; Martin III, ten; Dexter, seven; and four-year-old Bernice with white ribbons in her hair) and looking like Jackie's veil-wearing shorter sister in grief, was forced similarly to plow through the agitated masses grouped out front. It was just the beginning of a very long, hot, solemn, sad, and somewhat surreal day.

Pulitzer Prize–winning historian David Levering Lewis, in his *King: A Biography*, describes Martin's last rites as "protracted, elaborate, and fussily confused." He vividly captures the unhappy mix of not wholly welcome white politicians making appearances for political purposes and a genuinely mournful and outraged black community: "Crushed together in the narrow pews, pinned against the walls, and sweating terribly in the sticky heat of the church, the white politicians and public figures almost earned the credibility they sought that day. But they were made to pay dearly for it, for, thanks to [King's Southern Christian Leadership Conference successor] Ralph Abernathy, the service went along interminably. Finally, at 12:15 P.M., the ordeal ended and the sweltering three-and-a-half-mile march to Morehouse College began. . . . The mule cart bearing the remains of the fallen leader was almost capsized by the excitable crowd as it stood before the speakers' platform behind Atlanta University's administration building. . . . Singers without talent warbled the favorite hymns of the deceased, while the merciless Georgia sun beat down upon the gathering of fifty thousand."

In a dignified effort to keep show business out of the proceedings, the funeral's featured singers were all, indeed, culled from the ranks of Ebenezer's choir. It was a tasteful and appropriate way to keep the focus on King, his work, and his church, but it was nevertheless a musical plan that didn't generate much excitement or emotion. Aretha Franklin was present, but she did not sing, notwithstanding numerous mistaken accounts that have proliferated over the years that she did. Aretha recalls visiting Coretta Scott King on her bed after the service and sitting in silence across from Leontyne Price on a shuttle bus that day in Atlanta. But she gave no performance.

The march from Ebenezer to Morehouse College, where sung and spoken tributes to Martin were scheduled to continue throughout the afternoon, had in fact started early. Atlantans crushed by having been unable to get close to the church staged a minirevolt by initiating the procession several hours early. Bomb threats necessitated a change in route, which wreaked havoc on a city ill equipped to cope with the historic moment, even if everything had gone according to plan. With thousands already en route, King's casket was placed onto a mule-pulled cart fitted with enormous wooden wagon wheels, which aligned Martin in his final public moments with the struggling underclasses he had made it his life's work to champion. The reverend's colleagues—Abernathy, Andrew Young, Belafonte—walked alongside the vehicle clad in denim jeans and jackets, an outfit intended to give these men an air of salt-of-the-earth authenticity in tribute to Martin's Poor People's Campaign but which must have been awfully hot on this humid day and which had the somewhat disconcerting effect of making Martin Luther King's successors look like some sort of chain gang.

Abernathy served as master of ceremonies at the Morehouse service as well, and though he was commanding, seeming in fact to relish to some degree the spotlight he had attracted via this tragic route, the program nevertheless moved along tentatively. Musically, this second service was scarcely more compelling than the first. More moving than the actual sung tributes was the sight of choir members wiping away tears from beneath their sixties cat-eye glasses between songs. One of the soloists was overcome midsong, dissolved into tears, and slumped back down in her chair. As Lewis puts it, "Even Mahalia failed to spark the assembly."

But a few weeks later, at an emotional, televised SCLC convention in Memphis, there was a musical performance, a memorial to Dr. King, that summoned the expansive, emotion-driven plane of coexisting anguish and ecstasy that *is* gospel music at its finest, and that did succeed in sparking the assembly. Aretha Franklin sang in Martin's memory, performing his favorite gospel standard, the Thomas Dorsey–penned "Precious Lord, Take My Hand." She wore a simple off-white dress, a small gold cross hanging around her neck. It was still 1968, and Aretha had yet to shun the big hair and dramatic, inky eye makeup that she had sported just two months earlier, the last time she sang for Martin, on Aretha Franklin Day. King had given her a special Southern Christian Leadership Conference award to honor and thank her for the numerous performances she had given (often sharing a bill with Dick Gregory, Nipsey Russell, or Belafonte) on the group's behalf.

Now she was returning the favor, if you could call it that, delivering a profoundly felt, time-stopping rendition of the song. Sweat dripped from her temples, true emotion was in her face. As she had been taught by her father (another reverend who would die young, shot by burglars in his Detroit home in 1979, after which he lay in a coma for five years before finally succumbing), Aretha took her time with the song, infusing each lyric with meaning, letting each musical phrase hang in the air, gleaming and perfect, for the audience to observe and appreciate. When she sang the words, "precious Lord, take my hand/lead me on, let me stand/I am tired, I am weak, I am worn," she was speaking for every American who had been touched or affected by King's crusade and who now had to ponder continuing without him.

She certainly spoke for Coretta King, who once more was seated in the front pew, again in black but this time veilless, a burgundy bow affixed to her suit jacket. Again, her kids sat with her, though not in the formal attire they had worn at the funeral. As Aretha sang to King's widow and her four youngsters, it's hard to imagine that she failed to think of her own three sons (the fourth not yet born). Clarence and Eddie were roughly the same age as Martin III and Dexter, a fact that couldn't have escaped Aretha's notice as she looked into their faces gazing up at her while she memorialized their father in song. Indeed, Aretha was singing for Martin; but even more so, she was singing for Coretta and the children, woman to woman, mother to mother.

Perhaps it makes sense that such otherwise thorough and accurate writers and sources as Jerry Wexler, *Time* magazine, and numerous others portrayed Aretha's version of "Precious Lord" as the highlight of King's actual funeral service at Ebenezer. It is understandable that documentarians would be thus mistaken, for what everyone sought in the aftermath of King's assassination were answers, hope, balm. And where better to turn for a restoration of one's faith in humanity than the mysterious well of human emotion that was Aretha Franklin's voice? Film critic Pauline Kael revealed part of the essence of Aretha's talent in a comparison of the singer to Billie Holiday. Billie, genius that she was, nevertheless had a voice that seemed the embodiment of suffering and heartache. Aretha, on the other hand, Kael argued, had the power to heal with her voice, to provide answers, to soothe frayed nerves, to restore one's faith in times of tribulation.

Indeed, that's what Aretha does when she sings gospel: she heals. Three years later, with the release of her sublime live gospel album *Amazing Grace,* Aretha would make a mainstream audience familiar with what the *New York Times* has called "the ecstatic, soaring spirit of the Baptist and Pentecostal traditions that shaped Miss Franklin's singing style. The very notion of a slow, teasing buildup to a delirious climax, the incessant repetition of textural and musical phrases, the flatted notes and the shivering ornamentation, the joyful choral responses—all these are integral to black gospel singing." As she sang her widely broadcast "Precious Lord" in honor of Martin, a slew of network microphones poking up at her from a podium, Aretha was showing America the power of the black church that King had come from. Aside from the tragic circumstances surrounding the performance, it must have been shocking for those unfamiliar with Aretha's gospel background to have witnessed. But it nevertheless provided a context for that novel fervor that had been unleashed on the world a year before with *I Never Loved a Man the Way I Love You.*

Martin's killing is widely cited as the cause of the demise of the black-and-white-produced soul music that Aretha brought to new heights and presented to a larger swath of listeners. With *I Never Loved a Man the Way I Love You,* Aretha had set new standards for the soul genre and for pop music as a whole. With her performance of "Precious Lord," she was memorializing not just King but the very musical form she'd just conquered and reinvented. Martin was dead, R&B could no longer be counted as a symbol of races coming together musically; an angrier, more pessimistic era was dawning, and people could feel it. But Aretha could provide abatement for that growing sense of disquiet. As she sang King's favorite gospel hymn, the same song she first recorded as a fourteen-year-old at New Bethel Baptist, the general fear of a social and emotional tumult was eased.

"She certainly has been a beacon," Nikki Giovanni told me. "I mean, there are ships out there, and she's been the lighthouse. And it's been good. Because some of us do crash. But it's nice to know where the lighthouse is. That's a line of mine: 'I need Aretha.' And it's good. Because that period of time in America, people needed a voice. And King was certainly one voice. And Aretha was another."

When asked to describe Aretha Franklin's singing voice, Jerry Wexler doesn't hesitate to find the right adjective: "It's ecstatic," he told me. "She finds ecstasy in herself and releases it. And that's what you hear. Better than anybody. That's who she was." As such, Franklin is like a kind of modern-day, soul-music Teresa of Avila, the sixteenth-century saint famously visited by angels and sent into spiritual raptures. When Aretha Franklin sings, she, too, is quite literally in ecstasies, outside herself, taken to a new zone—in gospel parlance, she gets happy, and she takes us there with her. Aretha has said, "I never left the church. The church goes with me." What the *New York Times* has called her "fearless, unbridled emotionalism" doesn't always come out in the Queen of Soul's performances, but it is always there, simmering under the surface if not entirely apparent. "She'll always be dangerous," Marvin Gaye once said of Aretha, fully aware of the musical glory at her disposal if she chose to use tap into it. "Ecstatic," says Jerry Wexler. "The music in her is perfect, natural, and untrammeled."

epilogue

Aretha's Vocal Art

*E*cstatic. Dangerous. Smokey. Airy. It's hard to describe Aretha's voice because so many adjectives apply. Hers is a wide-ranging voice that limns so many facets of feeling, that when Aretha sings it's as if she's performing a kind of alchemy. "This is an earth voice," Nikki Giovanni told me, making it clear that a poet is most capable of describing something as intangible as a voice. "This is a voice of okra, this is a voice of manure. You know what I'm saying? This is a voice that has not only a sound but a smell and a depth. A taste. You *hear* Aretha, but you also lick your lips. It's a fantastic thing."

Fantastic in the true meaning of the word. But how does she do it? Why is it often said, without explanation, that Aretha has superb "natural technique"? Good singing is about getting out of the way of one's breath, riding a column of air that originates in the diaphragm, and letting that breath do the work: bending the breath at certain points, pinching it at others, occasionally imposing only a light-fisted grip over it, letting it almost spill out of the mouth into a diffuse, airy puddle of sound. It's a technique that allows opera singers to fill enormous halls with no amplification, relaxedly unfurling air from the gut and focusing it into a tone, sculpting it into words as it leaves the mouth.

This is what Aretha does. This is why, when she speaks her voice is light, breathy, sometimes difficult to hear, but when she sings she overpowers. Aretha's voice, though focused and strong, *is* breathy, airy, and it's this fluttery, girlish quality mingled with the fundamental imperative of literal breath, of breathing, that characterizes her singing. Her talent is dichotomous: playful and wise, sweet and salty, free—"untrammeled"—and yet controlled. The mystery of Aretha's voice is that it's always two things at once—at least. Aretha never *just* sounds pained; she sounds pained and hopeful. She never just sounds libidinous; she's libidinous and pragmatic. This is why one person can hear "Do Right Woman—Do Right Man" and think the singer sounds anguished, and another can hear the joy.

"Head, heart, and throat," Wexler says. "Aretha has all three." There are singers who can stand there and virtuosically tear through any song, but the talent is purely in the cords (certain big-voiced Broadway belters come to mind). Another singer may be an interpretive genius but with limited sheer vocal ability (Billie Holiday's sublime musicianship, despite her tiny range, is a prime example). Yet another might have an almost coldly intellectual approach to performance; a listener doesn't experience tremendous emotion but rather is impressed by the singer's command of the musical text. Aretha has mastery over all three of these possibilities of the vocal art. With soprano-register operatic coloratura exceptions, there are few arrangements of notes she cannot essay intelligently, musically, and emotionally. People were shocked when Franklin stood in for an ailing Luciano Pavarotti and sang Puccini's tenor aria "Nessun dorma" at the 1998 Grammy Awards. But where else could she turn for a challenge *other* than the realm of opera? The gospel-to-opera trajectory is unique to Aretha Franklin, but it is, oddly, not entirely surprising. "Aretha Franklin has created what can only be called gospel bel canto," opera critic Albert Innaurato wrote that year. In fact, she created it in the sixties.

"Four octaves," Aretha has slyly said of her voice, though musicological sticklers argue. Franklin's true range, her vocal comfort zone, is probably more like three, but she employs a deep, molasses chest register and a spinning soprano for dynamic effect. "What distinguished Miss Franklin from other women gospel singers," the *New York*

Times once declared, "was the sheer power of her voice, its high belting register pushed into the soprano range without the operatic tonal roundness of a trained soprano extension. This is not mere technical gibberish: It defines a way of singing common to most popular vocalists of our time. But Miss Franklin did it better than almost anyone. And unlike some, she has an upper extension, but she uses it for coloration." Every note Aretha sings is colored, whether it's firmly within the central spread of her voice or at its extremes, pushed up and high or released low in a sultry growl.

A Chinese-American pianist says he notices a "kinship between African-American spirituals and Chinese folk songs. Whenever I hear Aretha Franklin sing 'Amazing Grace,' I'm reminded of Chinese opera." This comparison makes a kind of perverse sense for western listeners, as Aretha Franklin sings in her own language. No one sings like Aretha Franklin; her vocal vernacular is hers alone. And yet it's worth remarking on the textural incisiveness of her interpretations. Because so much of Aretha's output is vividly informed by her gospel intensity, the clarity and aptness of her word-shading artistry is overlooked. When she wails, "How *could* you treat me so bad" on "I Never Loved a Man," the musical emphasis is straight out of the gospel tradition, so the singer's emphasis on "could" and what that dictional choice suggests—the sense that she feels galled, outraged, disbelieving that anyone would mistreat her—is underappreciated.

Aretha's improvisational word-choice betrays her status as an educated, middle-class Northern girl singing in a largely rural, Southern vernacular. When she sings, Aretha relies on "ain't's" and "baby's" and other Southern-black down-homeisms. But in interviews her language shows no signs of anything other than its middle-class roots. These two juxtaposed languages both come from the church. As gospel traces to spirituals traces to field hollers, Aretha becomes a black-cultural tabula rasa for the dispossessed. As the gospel church nurtures, educates, provides strength and order, Aretha becomes a symbol of success and stability in black America. Grounded in gospel, in the church she moves in two directions, bringing together listeners from both extremes. Aretha's gospel roots, her steeping in that tradition, link her to a U.S.-historical black identity; her gospel talent links her to everyone.

Different listeners respond to different qualities in Aretha's singing, and sometimes I'm surprised by which numbers folks cite as their favorite tunes. Nikki Giovanni told me that the song that really *gets* her—"to this day, if I put it on, I have to be in a really, really positive mood"—is "Going Down Slow," and I responded with silence. The song, off *Aretha Arrives*, is a bluesy vocal showcase, but not a track I'd select as one of Franklin's most powerful. In his book *Just My Soul Responding: Rhythm and Blues, Black Consciousness, and Race Relations,* the habitually neutral Brian Ward betrays emotion when he mentions "the gorgeous 'Angel.'" Carolyn Franklin's composition *is* a beautiful tune, but worthy of reverence above "I Never Loved a Man," "Skylark," "Mary, Don't You Weep," and, most of all, "Today I Sing the Blues"? Those are *my* songs. (Along with "River's Invitation," "Won't Be Long," "Maybe I'm a Fool," "How I Got Over," "Crazy He Calls Me," and "Do Right Woman.")

In an essay exploring the conundrum of writing about music, the impossible task of attaching words to an intangible art form, Roland Barthes devises a concept he calls "the grain of the voice," which he describes emphatically as, "the very precise space of *the encounter between a language and a voice.*" He goes on to explain that the grain is not just a voice's timbre but also its significance. "The 'grain' is the body in the voice as it sings," he writes. Barthes's analysis is aimed specifically at the singing of German lieder. But this notion of timbre plus significance, sound plus context, technique, and the feeling it engenders, strikes me as a perfect way to explain (or at least attempt to) the uncanny aural-emotional appeal of Aretha Franklin's voice. The sheer sound grips us as listeners; the meaning of what she sings—both the literal lyrical text of her songs and their unspeakable, unclassifiable emotional underpinnings—keeps us in her thrall. Music and meaning—it's this marriage that makes Aretha's music important; and it's the fact that such an intellectualization pales alongside the purely emotional force of Aretha's work that makes her artistry not just important but vital. "I *need* Aretha," people say.

It's easier to just listen. "A woman's only human—this you should understand." "I want to be free, to fly away and sing to the world." "I don't know why I let you do these things to me." "Those who love always give the most." "You're the one I need—I don't want a love that's second best." "It might be one o'clock and it might be three. I don't care 'cause time means nothing to me." "R-E-S-P-E-C-T: Find out what it means to me!" Writing about Aretha's voice, words tend to fail, though Aretha's voice—her sound and her words—never do. Her voice may have been at its height in 1967, but its glory remains in tact. And in a business where so many women artists have succumbed early to the pressures, both professional and emotional—Bessie, Billie, Dinah—Aretha remains a survivor, a woman borne up by her faith and her talent. And those who *need* her are borne up too, by Aretha Franklin's unique and beautiful head, heart, and throat.

selected discography

I Never Loved a Man the Way I Love You remains, for me, Aretha's supreme achievement. It is the work that first announced her genius and that changed the rules of the pop game. But her catalogue is rich with other strong albums, interesting albums, and out-and-out masterpieces. Below is the bulk of her output (there have been so many various greatest hits sets that it would be foolish to list them all). I've included a few words about certain more significant recordings (and some personal favorites). Many of these albums are available on CD; other, more obscure releases, mainly from the Columbia years, require flipping through the bins at used-record shops or surfing on eBay. (Note that Columbia continued to release albums of back-stocked Aretha material for a few years after she had her first successes on Atlantic.)

VARIOUS LABELS

YOU GROW CLOSER (also known as *Precious Lord*)
1956

Aretha's teen gospel recording form her father's New Bethel Baptist Church has been released in various incarnations by various companies. The two most easily available are Universal Music's *You Grow Closer* (or *Precious Lord*) from Delta Entertainment, both of which have the same track listing. First hearing a breathtakingly precocious fourteen-year-old Aretha sing "Precious Lord" is like first encountering Little Stevie Wonder or baby Michael Jackson. She wasn't a widely recognized child star, per se, but the future Queen of Soul was a bona fide artist from a young age.

COLUMBIA RECORDS

THE GREAT ARETHA FRANKLIN: THE FIRST 12 SIDES (originally titled *Aretha*)
1961

I'm frankly surprised that this album didn't take off and launch Aretha into stardom immediately. Despite the constant chatter about her marginal Columbia work, this record marks a fabulous start. From "Won't Be Long" to "Maybe I'm a Fool" to "Today I Sing the Blues" to Gershwin's "It Ain't Necessarily So," the gospel feeling is there, making one wonder to what degree the label clamped down on Aretha's natural style. "Over the Rainbow" doesn't have the force of Judy Garland's iconic take of the song, but it illustrates teen Aretha's eclectic tastes.

THE ELECTRIFYING ARETHA FRANKLIN
1962

Who else could make a white-bread tune like "Ac-cent-tchu-ate the Positive" sound like the funkiest thing going? (Her run, late in the track, on the word "eliminate," which she stretches to ten rapid-fire syllables is probably the closest Harold Arlen ever got to gospel.) This album is also notable for its inclusion of the Reverend James Cleveland's song "Nobody Like You," which Aretha—perhaps because of her close relationship with Cleveland—seems particularly attached to and inspired by.

THE TENDER, THE MOVING, THE SWINGING ARETHA FRANKLIN
1962

LAUGHING ON THE OUTSIDE
1963

UNFORGETTABLE—A TRIBUTE TO DINAH WASHINGTON

1964

Aretha raced into the studio to record this tribute to one of her chief idols just weeks after Washington's death from a combination of alcohol and sleeping pills. Nat "King" Cole and, later, his daughter Natalie, are widely associated with this song; Franklin's version is typically unique and an exercise in how to build a vocal performance from soft, contained beginnings into a full-throttle gospel climax.

RUNNIN' OUT OF FOOLS

1964

This was the Clyde Otis–produced album that was supposed to bring Ree some hits. The record was promoted as a foray into R&B, which is comical alongside the gutbucket soul Aretha would unleash on Atlantic three years later. Still, it's fun to hear Aretha sing light, midsixties soul-pop fare like "Walk on By," "You'll Lose a Good Thing" and "The Shoop Shoop Song."

YEAH! ARETHA FRANKLIN IN PERSON

1965

SOUL SISTER

1966

TAKE IT LIKE YOU GIVE IT
1967

TAKE A LOOK
1967

SOFT AND BEAUTIFUL
1969

SWEET BITTER LOVE
1970

ARETHA AFTER HOURS
1976

ARETHA SINGS THE BLUES
1980

JAZZ TO SOUL
1992

THE QUEEN IN WAITING
2003

Columbia periodically releases a new greatest hits package of Franklin's early work, and this recent product is one of the best. The previously unreleased alternate take (one of six such newly hearable tunes) of "Bill Bailey, Won't You Please Come Home" is a bubbly treat. Now if only the label would release a collection with *all* of Franklin's magic versions of "Skylark" (this one features two).

ATLANTIC RECORDS

I NEVER LOVED A MAN THE WAY I LOVE YOU
1967

ARETHA ARRIVES
1967

LADY SOUL
1968

Aretha knocked out another album in 1967 straight on the heels of *I Never Loved a Man* (*Aretha Arrives*, which features "Baby, I Love You" and a cover of the Rolling Stones' "Satisfaction"), but the true second act to her Atlantic debut is *Lady Soul*, released in January 1968 and proving beyond question that the Queen of Soul truly deserved her mantle. "Chain of Fools" remains one of the most popular songs in her catalogue. Eric Clapton's guitar filigree elevates "Good to Me As I Am to You," which, though not a well-known track, certainly ranks among Aretha's best, most impassioned vocal performances. And then, of course, there's "(You Make Me Feel Like) A Natural Woman," perhaps Aretha's most recognizable song after "Respect" and a perfect expression of her musical personality.

ARETHA NOW
1968

ARETHA IN PARIS
1968

SOUL 69
1969

Soul 69 doesn't generally get a lot of ink, but it's an interesting kind of pivot from Aretha's first five Atlantic albums (which are characterized by short, tight, bursting blasts of soul) to her next five (which are more conceptual and feature longer tracks that seem slightly less aimed at the pop charts). She slows down and adds a verse to her redo of "Today I Sing the Blues." "Bring It on Home to Me"—with its blasting horns, jazzy vibe, and full-throttle vocals—sounds nothing like Sam Cooke's original. And "Crazy He Calls Me" is an Atlantic-era reminder of Aretha's gift for jazz and an absolute vocal marvel.

THIS GIRL'S IN LOVE WITH YOU

1970

This is the first release of what could be called Aretha's mature period at Atlantic. Whether Paul McCartney originally wrote "Let It Be" for Franklin or not, she seizes control of the song on this version (the climactic progression where she sings, "Let it be, let it be, let it be—leave it a*lone*—let it be" is chilling). "Dark End of the Street," written by Penn and Moman, who also penned "Do Right," makes one wish Franklin had recorded even more of their songs. She puts her own, slow Southern-soul spin on Dusty Springfield's iconic "Son of a Preacher Man" (Franklin had first dibs on the song a few years earlier but passed, to Dusty's eternal benefit). And "Call Me," written by Aretha, is one of her most personal tracks: Jimmy Johnson recalls that she was crying on the studio floor while recording the vocal. "The tears were splashing onto the music stand."

SPIRIT IN THE DARK

1970

I asked Jerry Wexler if *I Never Loved a Man* were his favorite Aretha Franklin record, and he hesitated: "*Spirit in the Dark* is a motherfucker." It's true. From the opening piano chords of the Ahmet Ertegun–penned "Don't Play That Song for Me" (originally recorded by Ben E. King) to the relaxed vocal and killer piano work of "Pullin" and the sexy-spiritual title track, this album captures the mature Aretha at the apex of her Atlantic association. With six studio albums behind her, the formula was firmly established and Aretha could freely express herself as an adult artist with a firm grip on her musical vision.

LIVE AT FILLMORE WEST

1971

Aretha conquers the flower children, as Wexler puts it, in this live concert recorded at San Francisco's Fillmore Theater. Soft-rock group Bread is funky for the first (and maybe only) time on Aretha's rendition of "Make It with You;" Ray Charles shows up for an encore of "Spirit in the Dark;" "Reach Out and Touch Somebody's Hand" makes Diana Ross's version sound sung by a different species. The highpoint: a seven-minute "Dr. Feelgood" that Aretha turns into an out-and-out church service, with the most fervent gospel coda she's ever slapped on a pop tune.

YOUNG, GIFTED AND BLACK

1972

AMAZING GRACE

1972

Recorded with Clara Ward in the audience and James Cleveland at the piano, this double album live gospel recording at the New Temple Missionary Baptist Church in Los Angeles is rightly considered Aretha's gospel masterpiece and one of the highlights of her career. Church staples like Ward's "How I Got Over," Thomas A. Dorsey's "Precious Lord, Take My Hand," and a ten-minute, freeform "Amazing Grace" are interspersed with gospel takes on quasi-spiritual pop fare, like Marvin Gaye's "Wholly Holy," Carole King's "You've Got a Friend," and Rodgers and Hammerstein's "You'll Never Walk Alone." Highlight number one: the piercing duet with Reverend Cleveland on "Precious Memories." Highlight number two: spoken remarks from Aretha's father, Reverend C. L. Franklin.

HEY NOW HEY (THE OTHER SIDE OF THE SKY)

1973

LET ME IN YOUR LIFE

1974

WITH EVERYTHING I FEEL IN ME

1974

YOU
1975

SPARKLE
1976

After a three-year slump, Aretha returns to form with this all Curtis Mayfield–penned album of songs from the film of the same title.

SWEET PASSION
1977

ALMIGHTY FIRE
1978

LA DIVA
1979

ARISTA RECORDS

ARETHA
1980

LOVE ALL THE HURT AWAY

1981

JUMP TO IT

1982

All of a sudden, forty-year-old Franklin was popular again, proving she could still have an impact on the charts with the Luther Vandross–produced title track.

GET IT RIGHT

1983

WHO'S ZOOMIN' WHO?

1985

If *Jump to It* announced Aretha's return a few years earlier, this album returned the singer to superstar status. "Sisters Are Doin' It for Themselves," the duet with Annie Lennox, makes Ree a feminist icon all over again. And "Freeway of Love," a number-three pop hit, proved that in her forties Aretha could still add classic signature songs to her repertoire.

ARETHA

1986

ONE LORD, ONE FAITH, ONE BAPTISM

1987

THROUGH THE STORM

1989

WHAT YOU SEE IS WHAT YOU SWEAT

1991

A ROSE IS STILL A ROSE

1998

Another return to form after another slump of sorts. Lauryn Hill produced the rollingly funky title track, on which a fifty-six-year-old Aretha (!) somehow manages to sound girlish at the same time as wise and experienced. Just another in the ongoing series of surprises in Ree's career and proof that she can essay contemporary material even as a middle-aged woman.

SO DAMN HAPPY

2003

acknowledgments

Just as making an album requires untold participants, so does writing about one. Chief among my collaborators was my wonderful editor, Elizabeth Beier, who demonstrated much-appreciated enthusiasm, well-timed encouragement, and, above all, supreme patience. Thank you as well to all her St. Martin's Press colleagues. My agent, Scott Waxman, provided invaluable assistance in the early stages as we developed the idea for the book. (Plus, he sold it.) Everyone I interviewed about Aretha's life and career was remarkably forthcoming and friendly. I'd like to give special thanks to Jerry Wexler, who couldn't have been more helpful, insightful, funny, generous, and flat-out gung-ho on the project. Industry legends and compatriots Ahmet Ertegun and Arif Mardin graciously shared their recollections of the Queen of Soul in her prime. I love the

Muscle Shoals "boys" and the Memphians who worked on *I Never Loved a Man;* without exception, they're brilliant musicians and stirring raconteurs: Rick Hall, Spooner Oldham, Dan Penn, Jimmy Johnson, Chips Moman, Roger Hawkins, David Hood, and Charlie Chalmers. Thanks also to Rodney Hall and Daniel Beard of Fame. I had a great conversation with Ted White, who was very encouraging and who gave me a much fuller picture of Aretha's artistic process than I'd had. Clyde Otis also had valuable recollections, as did Representative Louise Bishop and Phyl Garland. David Ritz, having coauthored both Aretha's and Wexler's autobiographies, had a fascinating and often hilarious point of view on their work together. I'm enormously grateful to Nikki Giovanni for applying her own poetry to describing Aretha's and for contributing so much to this project. Thanks are in order to her associate, Virginia Fowler, as well. Thanks to George Hodgman for the original germ of the idea. The staffs of the King Center in Atlanta, the Schomburg Center for Research in Black Culture, and the Museum of Television and Radio provided assistance that I very much appreciated. I'd like to thank the Michael Ochs Archive and photographer David Gahr for the truly great photos. Ellis Levine provided valuable legal advice. On a personal note, my parents, Josephine and Paul Dobkin, gave me tremendous support during the writing of this book. I'm also grateful to Allyson Pimentel for her help emotional and otherwise and for reading early pages. Charles Runnette was an instrumental presence in the early weeks and months of the project. Lee Phillips was an insightful sounding board as well as a great listener. I'm indebted to Brooke Runnette, Tisa Coen, Alex Ceglia, Sidaya Moore, and Kippy Joseph. And finally I'd like to thank Aretha Franklin, a presence not just in these pages, but in my life since I first heard *I Never Loved a Man*.

Index